beauty in the ordinary

an inspiring collection of readings and meditations for Lent or any time

Rev. Samuel Johnson Lindamood, Jr.

Edited by Rev. Dr. Wesley J. Wildman

Copyright © 2020 Wesley J. Wildman

Edited by Wesley J. Wildman

Published by Wildhouse Publications. No part of this book may be reproduced in any manner without the written permission from the publisher, except in brief quotations embodied in critical articles or reviews. Contact info@wildhousepublications.com.

Printed in the USA

All Rights Reserved

Print ISBN 978-1-7360750-0-5
e-Book ISBN: 978-1-7360750-3-6

For Ann, Robin, Wendy,
Peggy, and Missy

editor's introduction

Lent is a time for taking stock of one's life, a time of reflection and restructuring. Most of us need help to accomplish this, and that's how the genre of the Lenten Manual of Discipline was born. Of course, nobody talks that way anymore; manuals of discipline are for legal proceedings, not matters of the spirit. But the idea still makes sense to anyone who has tried to break a habit or forge a new one.

Beauty in the Ordinary is probably the most distinctive Lenten manual of discipline ever created. It is contemporary, accessible, practical, and benefits from the spiritual genius of its author, Rev. Samuel Johnson Lindamood, Jr. It includes substitute days in case you don't like something you read and instructions for use at other times of the year, not just Lent. It is thoughtfully illustrated and capable of helping you see the world differently, each and every day.

As you use this book to deepen your spiritual perception, I want you to understand something of the person who wrote the daily meditations and selected most of the accompanying readings. Sam, or "Big Sam" as he was often called due to his impressive height, was a dynamic preacher and gifted pastor whose ministry in Arizona and California churches nurtured and transformed generations of people. He believed that preaching was the expression of personality in relation to religious themes and he was a master of the craft. That same combination of proclamation and personality is abundantly evident in the pages of this book.

Sam intuitively grasped the ambiguity of religion, which helped him communicate with its cultured despisers. He was able to convey the benefits of religion without artificially or falsely idealizing it. He stood for tolerance and inclusiveness and against bigotry and fanaticism—including religious bigotry and fanaticism. That was vital for me when I was Sam's junior colleague and mentee. He was important to me in a way that defies words. Many would say the same. We were privileged to know him.

When I worked with Sam in Piedmont, California, I saw first-hand how intimately his loving presence was woven into the lives of hundreds of families through baptisms and weddings, through hospital visits in times of sickness and funerals when tragedy struck. Piedmont was a bedroom community for San Francisco corporate boardrooms, and numerous executives carried Sam's wise brand of kindness and generosity with them into complex business decisions, as they sought to live out their faith at the helms of companies that influenced the fates of countless people. They trusted Sam to tell them the truth even—no, especially—when it hurt. And they relied on him to stand beside them when a marriage fell apart or a child died or life just stopped making sense.

Sam wrote the meditations in the late 1980s. In 1990, I edited and laid out an unillustrated version of the book so that it could be bound and distributed to Sam's friends and followers. I have always been convinced that this way of engaging the Lenten season has a much wider potential audience and am grateful for the opportunity to bring it to those who need help taking Lent seriously but for whom existing resources are alienating or irrelevant. This version of the book is my attempt to honor Sam 30 years after he finished it, as the 25th anniversary of his death approaches. To those of you who need a less conventional, more practical approach to Lenten reflection, let Sam's words inspire you.

"Lent is one of my favorite times of the year. In a culture consumed with consuming, it seems that more is never enough. The eyes search for new and exciting sights, the appetite longs for more and varied tastes. A popular song of some years ago said it well: 'I can't get no satisfaction.' Lent offers a time to overcome our consumerism, to give up something as a discipline—not a popular idea, but an important one. Lent offers a time also of taking something on, some new and different commitment, perhaps. And, finally, Lent offers a time of meditation and reflection. This book is for meditation and reflection during the forty days of Lent, once per day. Perhaps someone 'taking it on' will be better able 'to give up something' or deepen their commitment."

Sam was a voracious reader. To accompany his meditations, he chose readings from some of his favorite books and paired

them with Bible passages. He wrote, "It is from the sorts of readings in this book, scriptural and otherwise, that my sermons, talks, and pastoral work have germinated. I am grateful for each one." He was modest about the spiritual value of his meditations: "I hope the reader will find them helpful and stimulating. If a few of the readings or my statements are provocative, let me remind the reader that these are one man's opinion. One of my favorite quotes is, 'De gustibus non est disputandum' (there is no disputing of taste). What's good for one may not be good for another. I always hope that what I have found helpful will not offend someone else but I know that it will probably happen, given such different tastes among us. These also are my present conclusions; I still claim the privilege and openness of changing my mind."

Sam didn't live long enough to change his mind. Soon after he finished this book, the Oakland Firestorm of 1991 swept through the hills where he and his wife, Ann, lived. That fire destroyed their home and all their possessions. They narrowly escaped with their dog and their lives. Everything Sam had ever said from the pulpit or at the hospital bedside about the futility of using things we can own to protect ourselves from our finitude was confirmed in his own experience. Always a person of peace, Sam discovered a new and deeper joy after that experience. But, tragically, a few years later, he was struck low by brain tumors. As is often the case, the pain and personality changes associated with brain cancer were difficult to bear, but his faith kept him strong.

Sam Lindamood with grandson Andy Rico

My last visit with Sam before he died was at first a quiet conversation and then a very slow walk around the block, as we recalled for one another our habit of walking together around the town where we once served as ministers. He leaned heavily on me and one of his daughters as we walked, concentrating on making each step a safe one. In that extended moment of togetherness, we said our goodbyes. He left so many traces in my life and the lives of many others. In particular, this book became a precious memento of his character and wisdom for those fortunate enough to possess a copy of it. Now that fortunate group includes you.

May you have a blessed Lent in the company of Rev. Samuel Johnson Lindamood, Jr.

Rev. Dr. Wesley J. Wildman

contents

The Forty Days of Lent

1 – repetitive regrets
2 – what is real?
3 – running away from it all
4 – what does it mean to be a person?
5 – loneliness
6 – check your escalator
7 – the awesome nature of freedom
8 – believing impossible things
9 – some people are more equal than others
10 – the lusts that drive us
11 – different strokes for different folks
12 – crap-detecting
13 – a simple notion of being good
14 – no man is an island
15 – ready to go
16 – what is love?
17 – searchers
18 – the best things in the worst times
19 – finding meaning under any circumstances
20 – the therapy of breadbaking
21 – you can't go home again
22 – lip-smacking, exuberant delight
23 – facing your mortality
24 – single-minded not narrow-minded
25 – euphoric euthanasia
26 – there is hope in a burp
27 – dealing with the absurd
28 – new ways of seeing
29 – strangers and sojourners
30 – the human being awaits his besieger
31 – the great roles are prosaic
32 – unfreakability: the art of quieting the mind
33 – giving and receiving
34 – growing old gracefully
35 – the compassionate beast
36 – the will of god
37 – the wonder of grace
38 – the struggle for security knows no seasons
39 – wrestling through to god
40 – on keeping on keeping on

The Sundays in Lent

First Sunday in Lent
41 – the process of taming

Second Sunday in Lent
42 – the salt of the earth, not the honey of the hill

Third Sunday in Lent
43 – there is no separation

Fourth Sunday in Lent
44 – mysterium tremendum

Passion Sunday
45 – don't neglect the blood

Palm Sunday
46 – choosing means renouncing

Easter Sunday
47 – the miracle of metamorphosis

Substitute Days

Substitute Day 1
48 – the denizens of the night

Substitute Day 2
49 – when you can't find the tiger

Substitute Day 3
50 – beyond astonishment

for lent

The Days of Lent — Day

Ash Wednesday 1
    Thursday 2
    Friday 3
    Saturday 4

First Sunday of Lent (day 41)
    Monday 5
    Tuesday 6
    Wednesday 7
    Thursday 8
    Friday 9
    Saturday 10

Second Sunday of Lent (day 42)
    Monday 11
    Tuesday 12
    Wednesday 13
    Thursday 14
    Friday 15
    Saturday 16

Third Sunday of Lent (day 43)
    Monday 17
    Tuesday 18
    Wednesday 19
    Thursday 20
    Friday 21
    Saturday 22

The Days of Lent — Day

Fourth Sunday of Lent (day 44)
    Monday 23
    Tuesday 24
    Wednesday 25
    Thursday 26
    Friday 27
    Saturday 28

Fifth Sunday of Lent (day 45)
    Monday 29
    Tuesday 30
    Wednesday 31
    Thursday 32
    Friday 33
    Saturday 34

Palm Sunday (day 46)
    Monday 35
    Tuesday 36
    Wednesday 37
    Maundy Thursday 38
    Good Friday 39
    Saturday 40

Easter Sunday (day 47)

for pentecost

The Days of Pentecost — Day

Easter Sunday 1
    Monday 2
    Tuesday 3
    Wednesday 4
    Thursday 5
    Friday 6
    Saturday 7

First Sunday after Easter 8
    Monday 9
    Tuesday 10
    Wednesday 11
    Thursday 12
    Friday 13
    Saturday 14

Second Sunday after Easter 15
    Monday 16
    Tuesday 17
    Wednesday 18
    Thursday 19
    Friday 20
    Saturday 21

Third Sunday after Easter 22
    Monday 23
    Tuesday 24
    Wednesday 25
    Thursday 26
    Friday 27
    Saturday 28

The Days of Pentecost — Day

Fourth Sunday after Easter 29
    Monday 30
    Tuesday 31
    Wednesday 32
    Thursday 33
    Friday 34
    Saturday 35

Fifth Sunday after Easter 36
    Monday 37
    Tuesday 38
    Wednesday 39
    Thursday (Ascension Day) 40
    Friday 41
    Saturday 42

Sixth Sunday after Easter
(Sunday after Ascension) 43
    Monday 44
    Tuesday 45
    Wednesday 46
    Thursday 47
    Friday 48
    Saturday 49

Pentecost Sunday (Whitsunday) 50

a prayer to begin

Listen, Lord
O Lord, we come this morning
Knee-bowed and body-bent
Before thy throne of grace.
O Lord—this morning—
Bow our hearts beneath our knees,
And our knees in some lonesome valley.
We come this morning—
Like empty pitchers to a full fountain,
With no merits of our own.
O Lord--open up a window of heaven,
And lean out far over the battlements of glory,
And listen this morning.
And now, O Lord, this man of God,
Who breaks the bread of life this morning—
Shadow him in the hollow of thy hand,
And keep him out of the gunshot of the devil.
Take him, Lord—this morning—
Wash him with hyssop inside and out,
Hang him up and drain him dry of sin.
Pin his ear to the wisdom-post,
And make his words sledge hammers of truth—
Beating on the iron heart of sin.
Lord God, this morning—
Put his eye to the telescope of eternity,
And let him look upon the paper walls of time.
Lord, turpentine his imagination,
Put perpetual motion in his arms,
Fill him full of the dynamite of thy power,
Anoint him all over with the oil of thy salvation,
And set his tongue on fire.
And now, O Lord—
When I've done drunk my last cup of sorrow—
When I've been called everything but a child of God—
When I'm done travelling up the rough side of the mountain-
O—Mary's Baby—
When I start down the steep and slippery steps of death—
When this old world begins to rock beneath my feet—
Lower me to my dusty grave in peace
To wait for that great gittin' up morning—Amen.

James Weldon Johnson, God's Trombones

repetitive regrets **day 1**

A blur of romance clings to our notions of "publicans," "sinners," "the poor," "the people in the marketplace," "our neighbors," as though of course God should reveal himself, if at all, to these simple people, these Sunday school watercolor figures, who are so purely themselves in their tattered robes, who are single in themselves, while we now are various, complex, and full at heart. We are busy. So, I see now, were they. Who shall ascend into the hill of the Lord? Or who shall stand in his holy place? There is no one but us. There is no one to send, nor a clean hand, nor a pure heart on the face of the earth, nor in the earth, but only us, a generation comforting ourselves with the notion that we have come at an awkward time, that our innocent fathers are all dead—as if innocence had ever been—and our children busy and troubled, and we ourselves unfit, not yet ready, having each of us chosen wrongly, made a false start, failed, yielded to impulse and the tangled comfort of pleasures, and grown exhausted, unable to seek the thread, weak and involved. But there is no one but us. There never have been. There have been generations which remembered, and generations which forgot; there has never been a generation of whole men and women who lived well for even one day. Yet some have imagined well, with honesty and art, the detail of such a life, and have described it with such grace, that we mistake vision for history, dream for description, and fancy that life has devolved. So. You learn this studying any history at all, especially the lives of artists and visionaries; you learn it from Emerson, who noticed that the meanness of our days is itself worth our thought; and you learn it, fitful in your pew, at church.

Anne Dilliard, Holy The Firm

Almighty and most merciful Father; We have erred and strayed from thy ways like lost sheep. We have followed too much the devices and desires of our own hearts. We have offended against thy holy laws. We have left undone those things which we ought to have done; And we have done those things which we ought not to have done; And there is no health in us. But, thou, O Lord, have mercy upon us, miserable offenders. Spare thou those, O God, who confess their faults. Restore thou those who are penitent; According to thy promises declared unto mankind in Christ Jesus our Lord. And grant, O most merciful Father, for his sake; That we may hereafter live a godly, righteous, and sober life, To the glory of thy holy Name. Amen.

1928 U.S. Book of Common Prayer

Have mercy on me, O God,
according to thy steadfast love;
according to thy abundant mercy
blot out my transgressions.
Wash me thoroughly from my iniquity,
and cleanse me from my sin!
For I know my transgressions,
and my sin is ever before me.
Against thee, thee only, have I sinned,
and done that which is evil in thy sight,
so that thou art justified in thy sentence
and blameless in thy judgment.
Behold, I was brought forth in inequity,
and in sin did my mother conceive me.

Psalm 51:1-5

The Lord is merciful and gracious,
slow to anger
and abounding in steadfast love.
He will not always chide,
nor will he keep his anger forever.
He does not deal with us
according to our sins,
nor requite us according to our iniquities.
For as the heavens are high above the earth,
so great is his steadfast love
toward those that fear him;
as far as the east is from the west,
so far does he remove our
transgressions from us.

Psalm 103:8-12

day 1

I do not understand my own actions. For I do not do what I want, but I do the very thing I hate... So I find it to be a law that when I want to do right, evil lies close at hand. Wretched man that I am! Who will deliver me from this body of death?

Romans 7:15, 21, 24

If we say we have no sin, we deceive ourselves, and the truth is not in us. If we confess our sins, he is faithful and just, and will forgive our sins and cleanse us from all unrighteousness.

I John 1:8-9

Therefore, if any one is in Christ, he is a new creation; the old has passed away, behold, the new has come.

II Corinthians 5:17

day 1

REPETITIVE REGRETS

Some Christian traditions begin Ash Wednesday by making the sign of the cross in ashes upon the forehead of the believer and intoning the ancient words, "Ashes to ashes and dust to dust." It is a somber but powerful reminder of our mortality, which will be overcome on Easter Sunday by "the sure and certain hope of resurrection to eternal life through Jesus Christ our Lord." The in-between-days are given to us for reflection on who we are and what we are doing. Lent is a time for focusing more clearly on what we are meant to be, rather than what we have been.

We are so easily caught in our sins, our bad habits, our unhappy thoughts, our recalcitrant ways. Some years ago a country-western singer by the name of Eddie Rabbit had a hit tune entitled, "Repetitive Regrets." It was a fairly typical country-western song with its emphasis upon repetitive modes of behavior that bring personal sorrow and continuing regrets.

"Repetitive regrets" is a theme running through our lives. Over and over we experience what St. Paul expressed so poignantly: "That which I would, I do not and that which I would not, I do... Wretched man that I am! Who will deliver me from this body of death?" We may not be so dramatic or theological about it but most of us know the feeling. We have been there!

Our ways of expressing our inadequacy are legion. "Man, did I screw up." "I made a booboo." "I goofed!" "What a tragic mistake." "It's my fault! I'm sorry!" "Wrong, wrong, wrong!" "Oh, no, not again!" Guilt, guilt, guilt.

Guilt is such a major part of our experience. Parents are good at instilling guilt in their children; it is easier to control them that way. Churches are good at instilling guilt in their parishioners; it is easier to control them that way. Fundraising in America, sacred or secular, uses guilt as a primary motivational tool. Guilt makes us vulnerable to manipulation.

Few are those who can control their guilt. The couches of analysts and the offices of psychologists are full of people who don't know what to do with their guilt. Rationalization and projection are common words in our vocabulary now as a result of our need to deal with our guilt, our repetitive regrets.

The comedian, Flip Wilson, was immensely popular for a while with his funny way of saying, "The devil made me do it." The "devil-theory" has been used down through the centuries as a way of explaining why "we do the things we would not and do not do the things we would." Unfortunately, the theory doesn't work. Even if the devil made you do it, it is still your fault, and the regret is still there. "Wretched man that I am!"

Let us acknowledge that we enter Lent with "repetitive regrets," but let us at the same time acknowledge anew the grace of Jesus, whom Christians recognize as the Christ. Lent is a time to dwell on Christ's grace and not on our sin. Let us clean the slate! "If a person is in Christ, he or she is a new creation. The old is past and gone. Behold, the new is present." Thank God for the Assurance of Pardon, not just during Lent, but every day God gives us.

It's better than repetitive regrets.

what is real? day 2

"What is REAL?" asked the Rabbit one day, when they were lying side by side near the nursery fender, before Nana came to tidy the room. "Does it mean having things that buzz inside you and a stick-out handle?"

"Real isn't how you are made," said the Skin Horse. "It's a thing that happens to you. When a child loves you for a long, long time, not just to play with, but REALLY loves you, then you become Real."

"Does it hurt?" asked the Rabbit.

"Sometimes," said the Skin Horse, for he was always truthful. "When you are Real you don't mind being hurt."

"Does it happen all at once, like being wound up," he asked, "or bit by bit?"

"It doesn't happen all at once," said the Skin Horse. "You become. It takes a long time. That's why it doesn't happen to people who break easily, or have sharp edges, or who have to be carefully kept. Generally, by the time you are Real, most of your hair has been loved off, and your eyes drop out and you get loose in the joints and very shabby. But these things don't matter at all, because once you are Real you can't be ugly, except to people who don't understand."

"I suppose you are Real?" said the Rabbit. And then he wished he had not said it, for he thought the Skin Horse might be sensitive. But the Skin Horse only smiled.

"The Boy's Uncle made me Real," he said. "That was a great many years ago; but once you are Real you can't become unreal again. It lasts for always."

Margery Williams, The Velveteen Rabbit

Alice took up the fan and gloves, and, as the hall was very hot, she kept fanning herself all the time she went on talking. "Dear! Dear! How queer everything is today! And yesterday things went on just as usual. I wonder if I've been changed in the night? Let me think: WAS I the same when I got up this morning? I almost think I can remember feeling a little different. But if I'm not the same, the next question is, 'Who in the world am I?' Ah, THAT'S the great puzzle!" And she began thinking over all the children she knew that were of the same age as herself, to see if she could have been changed for any of them.

Lewis Carroll, Alice's Adventure In Wonderland

That I am a man,
this I share with other men.
That I see and hear and
that I eat and drink
is what all animals do likewise.
But that I am is only mine
and belongs to me
and to nobody else;
to no other man
not to an angel nor to God—
except inasmuch
as I am one with Him.

Master Meister Eckhart, Fragments

I think I could turn and live with animals,
they are so placid and self-contained,
I stand and look at them long and long.
They do not sweat and whine
about their condition,
They do not lie awake in the dark
and weep for their sins,
They do not make me sick
discussing their duty to God,
Not one is dissatisfied, not one is demented
with the mania of owning things,
Not one kneels to another, nor to his kind
that lived thousands of years ago,
Not one is respectable or unhappy
over the whole earth.

Walt Whitman, Song of Myself, 32

But to all received him, who believed in his name, he gave power to become children of God.

John 1:12

day 2

Beloved, let us love one another; for love is of God, and he who loves is born of God and knows God. In this the love of God was made manifest among us, that God sent his only Son into the world, so that we might live through him. In this is love, not that we loved God but that he loved us and sent his son to be the expiation for our sins. Beloved, if God so loved us, we also ought to love one another. No man has ever seen God; if we love one another, God abides in us and his love is perfected in us. By this we know that we abide in him and he in us, because he has given us of his own Spirit. And we have seen and testify that the Father has sent his Son as the Saviour of the world. Whoever confesses that Jesus is the Son of God, God abides in him, and he in God. So we know and believe the love God has for us. God is love, and he who abides in love abides in God, and God abides in him. In this is love perfected in us, that we may have confidence for the day of judgment.

I John 4:7-17a

Are there parts of your unique identity that you sometimes want to change to fit in or be accepted? Has anyone's love helped you to accept your real self, wounds and all?

day 2

WHAT IS REAL?

The philosophical world has long debated—What is real? Today's scientific community has great clashes between the realists (what you see is what you get) and the critical realists (it ain't necessarily so). But the question is hardest for you and me: What is real in our lives? What makes us real?

The Skin Horse had it right when he said what makes you real is "being loved." None of us is able to turn our stuffed animals into real ones by loving them, but almost; they are real to us. And we, like those stuffed animals, are most able to be real when we are with the people who love us. In their presence we feel most secure in letting go and just "being who we are."

Unfortunately, we also have moments of agreement with Kermit, the Frog, "It's not easy bein' green." Kermit wants to be a different color so he will stand out more; he doesn't want to be just ordinary, he wants to be flashy, but frogs are green, so he's stuck.

You and I often feel stuck, too. It's not always easy being who we are. We'd rather be someone else. We try to make ourselves into something other than we are. We would like to be exceptional; we would like to be different.

Seldom do we stop to think that differentness is what makes us who we are. To be different is part of the gift God gave each of us. Biological research today confirms how unique each of us is. We each have our own DNA and no one else has that particular DNA.

Research on the brain makes us realize that we are as different inside our heads as we are outside our heads. No wonder we see things differently than others. We are different, and that's good; or is it? Too often we do not affirm our uniqueness.

To know that you are different and to accept your differentness is a great step in the direction of knowing that you are real. Kermit is green like all frogs but he is different from all other frogs. You and I are *Homo sapiens* but we are different from all other *Homo sapiens*. Celebrate the difference; it is part of what makes you real.

In an image-conscious world we tend to confuse appearance with reality. Therefore, we have specialists in image-making. Politicians are elected by the images they convey. The cosmetic industry survives by helping people change their image, helping them where possible to look younger. Plastic surgeons get rich helping people change their appearance.

But changing the image doesn't change the reality. Rarely do we trust politicians because we know appearances are deceiving. Sad to say but most of our neighbors know who we are, even after plastic surgery and diets. What's real about you most likely has not changed to match the new image. Why do we continue to fool ourselves, then, about what is real?

Perhaps, because being loved and being different seems too simple and too difficult at one and the same time. How you look in the mirror will not help when someone challenges your worth. What will make a difference is when someone walks up to you and says, "I love you. You're different. You're special." Then you'll know—you're real!!

running away from it all **day 3**

Apparently, those of us who run do not all do it for the same reasons. Some are competitors, steadily increasing time and distance, entering races where runners can really hurt themselves, and reading *Runner's World*. Others are pure health freaks who never run any farther or faster, keep to the indoor track even when the sun shines, and talk about heartbeat rates and studies of longevity among runners. It seems that my crowd runs partly as an escape from the pressures of life. We're the ones for whom the change into ritual clothing, the pain of running, and the shower of cleansing constitute a daily rebaptism into newness of life. For us, the time spent running is time no one else has a claim on, and the rewards are similar to those of prayer and contemplation. Indeed, such exercise may constitute a secular pietism...

What these women were articulating [refers to a questionnaire asking women why they run] was the hope that running will save them from a state of helplessness. Incapacity at life's end is the new anxiety that modern medical technology has given Western society, and I am convinced that running has gained so many converts in recent years because people hope to guarantee that their bodies will not slowly decay in a modern "convalescent home." Runners want to remain active and independent until they die. Hidden somewhere in the pursuit of regular exercise is the notion that if one keeps moving, one will never be caught in the wires and tubes and sterile unprivacy that the aged suffer today.

D. William Faupel

Whither shall I go from thy Spirit?
Or whither shall I flee from thy presence?
If I ascend to heaven, thou art there!
If I make my bed in Sheol, thou art there!...
If I say, "let only darkness cover me,
and the light about me be night,"
even the darkness is not dark to thee ...
for darkness is as light with thee.

Psalm 139: 7-8, 11-12

When one of those who sat at table with him heard this, he said to him, "Blessed is he who shall eat bread in the kingdom of God!" But Jesus said to him, "A man once gave a great banquet, and invited many; and at the time for the banquet he sent his servant to say to those who had been invited, 'Come; for all is now ready.' But they all alike began to make excuses. The first said to him, 'I have bought a field, and I must go out and see it; I pray you, have me excused.' And another said, 'I have bought five yoke of oxen, and I go to examine them; I pray you, have me excused.' And another said, 'I have married a wife, and therefore cannot come.' So the servant came and reported this to his master. Then the householder in anger said to his servant, 'Go out quickly to the streets and lanes of the city, and bring in the poor and maimed and blind and lame.' And the servant said, 'Sir, what you commanded has been done, and still there is room.' And the master said to the servant, 'Go out to the highways and hedges, and compel people to come in, that my house may be filled. For I tell you, none of those men who were invited shall taste my banquet.'"

Luke 14:15-24

Do all things without grumbling or questioning, that you may be blameless and innocent, children of God without blemish in the midst of a crooked and perverse generation, among whom you shine as lights in the world, holding fast the word of life, so that in the day of Christ I may be proud that I did not run in vain or labor in vain... Not that I have already obtained this or am already perfect; but I press on to make it my own, because Christ Jesus has made me his own. Brethren, I do not consider that I have made it my own; but one thing that I do, forgetting what lies behind and straining forward to what lies ahead, I press on toward the goal for the prize of the upward call of God in Christ Jesus.

Philippians 2:14-16; 3:12-14

day 3

Are you running away from problems in your life? Can you stop to face them? Amidst the busyness of life, can you find time to slow down, look inside, and begin the race of faith?

day 3

RUNNING AWAY FROM IT ALL

America has become a nation of runners. Such a statement might seem more at home on the editorial pages of *Runner's World* but the kind of running of which I speak is much larger than the kind talked about in that esoteric magazine.

We run from ourselves, we run from others. We run from our worries and cares, we run from the future, we run from frustration, we run from responsibility, we run from our deepest feelings, we run from death. Like Chicken Little we are not always certain what we are running from, but why take the chance of getting hit on the head by a piece of sky? Run, Chicken Little, run. Run, you and me, run, run, run.

Childhood used to be a wonderful time of slowly learning how to get through life. It was acceptable for children to have time on their hands, to daydream, to be a little lazy, to dream about the future. Life goes so swiftly, the argument seemed to be, so why not let a child enjoy it.

Those days are gone forever. The "barefoot boy with cheek of tan" immortalized in James Whitcomb Riley's poem could not be written in today's world. There is too much for children to do, too much for children to learn. Hurry, hurry, run, run, run. If you don't run, you might miss something.

The Mad Hatter said it well for all of us:

"I'm late, I'm late,

For a very important date.

Can't even say hello, goodbye,

I'm late, I'm late, I'm late."

We joke about meeting ourselves as we come and go. Sad, but true.

What does it all mean—this running? Well, I suspect that's why we run. It may be too painful to sit down and ask the question of meaning. We might find out some things we don't want to know or don't want to think about. It might well call some of our life as we currently live it into question. That's why we run. As long as we can rationalize how busy we are, we never have to ask the question of meaning. Run, run, run.

Jesus told a poignant parable about those who would miss the banquet (the kingdom of God) because they are too busy. Each person had a perfectly acceptable excuse, even by today's standards. Each was an important person and had much to do. Too busy! Run, run, run. Don't stop to ask why, or what you might be missing!

Henry David Thoreau once wrote, "The mass of men lead lives of quiet desperation." Can you imagine what he would write today? We run from one thing to another—home, church, school, work, party, exercise, community responsibilities, children, spouse, parents, God. God??? How did God get in there? No time for that.

The Book of Hebrews says, "let us run with perseverance the race that is set before us, looking to Jesus the pioneer and perfecter of our faith." It's still running, but it surely is a different kind of race.

The rat race is a given. The race of faith is a possibility.

Our choice!

what does it mean to be a person? day 4

Life is not a state, it is a movement. Nowhere in nature does it present the character of a fixed and stable maximum, but rather of an undulation, successive waves of life. Sincerity, as we have seen, is not a perfected state, but a movement experienced just at the point at which one perceives that one lacks it. Love is not a state, it is a movement. Personal contact is not a state, but a fleeting movement that must be ceaselessly rediscovered.

Nor is spiritual life a state. Faith is a movement towards God, a turning back towards God which one feels at the very moment when one confesses that one has turned away. That is why Jesus Christ compared the spirit to the wind, of which one does not know 'whence it cometh, and whither it goeth,' to a force that passes, which cannot be laid hold of by the hands, and yet which quenches our thirst for the Absolute.

The person too is something that is uncompleted and evades our grasp. It imparts movement to our being, always refashioning our body and soul. The flowering of the person is not a state at which we arrive, it is the movement that results from perpetual incompleteness. If that flowering were the final stage of development, it would be also the halting of life. The rose that is in full bloom is already beginning to fade. Nor is the blossoming of the person, as so many people think, an accumulation of knowledge and experience, as if it were stones placed one upon another to form a monument. The only result of that would be a grandiose personage, not a person.

The person belongs to the realm of quality, not quantity. It is suddenly manifested in a powerful inner movement which partakes of the nature of the Absolute. However many things we accumulated, that would bring us no nearer to it. The person resides in being, not in having. It is beyond all measure; it eludes every test. It is outside all definitions. The claim to self-knowledge is the surest road to a misunderstanding of self.

Paul Tournier, The Meaning Of Persons

All the world's a stage,
And all the men and women merely players:
They have their exits and their entrances;
And one man in his time plays many parts,
His acts being seven ages.
At first the infant,
Mewling and puking in the nurse's arms.
And then the whining school
boy, with his satchel
And shining morning face, creeping like snail
Unwillingly to school.
And then the lover,
Sighing like furnace, with a woeful ballad
Made to his mistress' eyebrow.
Then a soldier,
Full of strange oaths and bearded like the pard,
Jealous in honour, sudden and quick in quarrel,
Seeking the bubble reputation
Even in the canon's mouth.
And then the justice,
In fair round belly with good capon lined,
With eyes severe and beard of formal cut,
Full of wise saws and modern instances;
And so he plays his part.
The sixth age shifts
Into the lean and slipper'd pantaloon,
With spectacles on nose and pouch on side,
His youthful hose, well saved, a world too wide
For his shrunk shank; and his big manly voice,
Turning again toward childish treble, pipes
And whistles in his sound.
Last scene of all,
That ends this strange eventful history,
Is second childishness and mere oblivion,
Sans teeth, sans eyes, sans
taste, sans everything.

William Shakespeare, As You Like It

day 4

But to all who received him, who believed in his name, he gave power to become children of God; who were born, not of blood nor of the will of the flesh nor of the will of man, but of God.

John 1:12-13

Now there was a man of the Pharisees, named Nicodemus, a ruler of the Jews. This man came to Jesus by night and said to him, "Rabbi, we know that you are a teacher come from God; for no one can do these signs that you do, unless God is with him." Jesus answered him, "Truly, truly, I say to you, unless one is born anew, he cannot see the kingdom of God." Nicodemus said to him, "How can a man be born when he is old? Can he enter a second time into his mother's womb and be born?" Jesus answered, "Truly, truly, I say to you, unless one is born of water and the Spirit, he cannot enter the kingdom of God. That which is born of the flesh is flesh, and that which is born of the Spirit is spirit. Do not marvel that I said to you, 'You must be born anew.' The wind blows where it wills, and you hear the sound of it, but you do not know whence it comes or whither it goes; so it is with every one who is born of the Spirit.

John 3:1-8

And he called to him the multitude with his disciples, and said to them, "If any man would come after me, let him deny himself and take up his cross and follow me. For whoever would save his life will lose it; and whoever loses his life for my sake and the gospel's will save it. For what does it profit a man, to gain the whole world and forfeit his life? For what can a man give in return for his life?"

Mark 8:34-37

When do you feel like your most authentic self? Are there any activities you lose yourself doing, yet find yourself by performing?

day 4

WHAT DOES IT MEAN TO BE A PERSON?

"Sixty years old and not knowing what I am going to do when I grow up" is the way a lot of my friends feel; I feel that way. It is a healthy feeling, I believe, because it means my life will continue to be a journey, to be full of surprises, no matter what my age. We, my friends and I, are, I suppose, in the sixth stage of Shakespeare's analysis, not looking forward to the final scene if it has to be as he depicts it—"second childishness and mere oblivion."

Better to look back and recall the movement, the discovery, the adventure. Every time I counsel someone, I am in awe of what it takes to be a person, knowing that the search for the real self never ends unless we stop seeking. We play so many roles on the stage of life that it is hard to ferret out the true person. I am not sure whether I am "at my best" (the true me) as a son, or a husband, or a father, or a preacher, or a friend.

I sometimes feel "at my best" when I am helping another person through the valley of the shadow of death. Somehow their suffering overshadows myself and in serving them I am better. Is that my true self? Certainly it is the words of Jesus come true—"he who loses his life shall find it."

"The person," according to Tournier, "is suddenly manifested in a powerful inner movement which partakes of the nature of the Absolute." He writes about being struck by grace and finding our best selves in the experience. John 1:12-13 says: "But to all who received him, who believed in his name, he gave power to become children of God; who were born, not of blood, nor of the will of the flesh nor of the will of man, but of God."

How does that happen? I wish I could describe in simple words that which I know to be true—I am a child of God. I cannot tell you when it happened or exactly how it happened but the feeling is a very special one. We often overlook the privilege of belonging, of being loved by a family. Being a part of God's family carries equal weight—belonging frees us to be our better selves.

Losing one's self and finding one's self are, paradoxically, part of the same experience. In the early nineteenth century, Scottish preacher Thomas Chalmers delivered a great sermon entitled, "The Expulsive Power of a New Affection." He observed that to have a new love is to be so captivated that all else loses significance. The lover feels more complete and denies self for the joy of giving to the beloved.

It is, then, our larger commitments that ultimately determine who we are. We may never pin down the one true self, but our better selves will surface as we commit ourselves to larger causes. "For whoever would save his life will lose it; and whoever loses his life for my sake and the gospel's will save it."

Even in Shakespeare's sixth stage such a commitment will bring movement and quality to life and enable one, if necessary, to endure even Shakespeare's worst: "sans teeth, sans eyes, sans taste, sans everything"—sans everything, but God. God we cannot do without for "in him we live and move and have our being." It is in God's love that we discover the meaning of persons.

loneliness day 5

We live in a society in which loneliness has become one of the most painful human wounds. The growing competition and rivalry which pervade our lives from birth have created in us an acute awareness of our isolation. This awareness has in turn left many with a heightened anxiety and an intense search for the experience of unity and community. It has also led people to ask anew how love, friendship, brotherhood and sisterhood can free them from isolation and offer them a sense of intimacy and belonging...

But the more I think about loneliness, the more I think that the wound of loneliness is like the Grand Canyon - a deep incision in the surface of our existence which has become an inexhaustible source of beauty and self-understanding.

Therefore I would like to voice loudly and clearly what might seem unpopular and maybe even disturbing: The Christian way of life does not take away our loneliness; it protects and cherishes it as a precious gift. Sometimes it seems as if we do everything possible to avoid the painful confrontation with our basic human loneliness, and allow ourselves to be trapped by false gods promising immediate satisfaction and quick relief. But perhaps the painful awareness of loneliness is an invitation to transcend our limitations and look beyond the boundaries of our existence. The awareness of loneliness might be a gift we must protect and guard because our loneliness reveals to us an inner emptiness that can be destructive when misunderstood, but filled with promise for him who can tolerate its sweet pain...

The wound of loneliness in the life of the minister hurts all the more, since he not only shares in the human condition of isolation, but also finds that his professional impact on others is diminishing. The minister is called to speak to the ultimate concerns of life: birth and death, union and separation, love and hate. He has an urgent desire to give meaning to people's lives. But he finds himself standing on the edges of events and only reluctantly admitted to the spot where the decisions are made...

...a deep understanding of his own pain makes it possible for him to convert his weakness into strength and to offer his own experience as a source of healing to those who are often lost in the darkness of their own misunderstood feelings. This is a very hard call, because for a minister who is committed to forming a community of faith, loneliness is a very painful wound which is easily subject to denial and neglect. But once the pain is accepted and understood, a denial is no longer necessary, and ministry can become a healing service.

Henri J.M. Nouwen, The Wounded Healer

At least once in each year of my life, for almost as long as I can remember, it has been necessary for me to return to the sea. The living waters draw me back to their shores again and again. They seem to wish to show me that though they are ever changing, yet they never change. The ocean is both endlessly calm and disruptively turbulent, alternately quieting my own inner turmoil, while yet insistently warning me of the dark powers that lie unquiet beneath the water's surface, and my own.

Inevitably, if I remain open to the tidal rhythms, the sea puts me in touch with the ebb and flow of my own inner area of unrest, my rising struggles and intermittent surrender and release. My romance with the sea helps me to know both the importance of my own singularity, and the meaninglessness of my trivial being.

As the (Hasidic) saying goes, a man must have two pockets into which he can reach at one time or another according to his needs. In his right pocket he must keep the words: "For my sake was the world created." And in his left: "I am dust and ashes."

...I survey the sea. My vision defines the world. I am the master. Then, perhaps through God's eye, I look in on myself, as if high on hashish. The ocean's vastness is beyond belief. I see myself as a pitiful speck at the edge of a cosmic puddle, a miniscule moment deluding himself that he is in charge of

day 5

Eternity. It is terrible to be so helplessly alone. Longing burns in my aching chest, my eyes mist over.

At the edge of the sea, I am the last human being left. And too, I am the first man ever created. It is my ocean and my sky. I feel the power of my sovereignty. It is heartbreakingly lonely. It is only a moment, this time-out. Yet I cannot bear the awful feeling that it will last forever.

Each year this happens. I know that this experience is coming, without ever quite remembering how much anguish it will bring. Yet this is part of why I return to the sea, to put myself in touch once more with my terrible loneliness, to learn again that I must bear this. To remember that this pain is the same for us all, that it is each man's weakness and his strength.

Sheldon B. Kopp
If You Meet The Buddha On The Road, Kill Him!

All man's history is an endeavor to shatter his loneliness.

Norman Cousins

Now from the sixth hour there was darkness over all the land until the ninth hour. And about the ninth hour Jesus cried with a loud voice, "E'li, E'li, lama sabachthani?" that is, "My God, my God, why hast thou forsaken me?" And some of the bystanders hearing it said, "This man is calling Elijah." And one of them at once ran and took a sponge, filled it with vinegar, and put it on a reed, and gave it to him to drink. But the others said, "Wait, let us see whether Elijah will come to save him." And Jesus cried again with a loud voice and yielded up his spirit.

Matthew 27:45-50

day 5

LONELINESS

*"All the lonely people,
where do they all come from?
All the lonely people,
where do they all belong?"*

Those words from Eleanor Rigby, a Beatles' song of the 1960s, may well raise the most profound question of our day. Loneliness seems endemic to the human situation, yet there is no feeling or thought that brings more denial than loneliness. It is not a topic for polite conversation. Talking about loneliness brings feelings of loneliness so let's change the subject.

I used to believe that the Christian ministry is the most lonely of all professions, for reasons too many to enumerate. As the years have gone by, I have come to understand that all persons in their professions deal with loneliness; they just don't want to talk about it. The chances are that the more successful they are and the higher up the corporate ladder they have climbed, the lonelier they will be. Shakespeare in King Henry IV says, "Uneasy is the head that wears the crown." There is nothing lonelier than sitting on top of the heap, wondering about those trying to take your place.

I was both taught in seminary and told when I was a young associate minister that "you can't have close friends in the church." To have close friends is to risk creating jealousies and unnecessary problems. To have close friends is to heighten the sense of rejection when you move to another parish; therefore, no friends allowed. No wonder ministers are lonely.

Thank God I did not believe that. The Lord has blessed me with many good friends, but that has little to do with my feelings of loneliness. If I talk about loneliness, my family and friends tend to laugh; there's no way I could be lonely—I'm too gregarious.

Loneliness has little to do with being alone. The loneliest times are in the midst of a group of people when you feel like you don't belong. The greatest loneliness occurs when the people who love you the most understand you the least. The greatest loneliness is to be rejected by someone whose opinion doesn't matter to you.

In these latter years I have learned to reclaim my quieter self, to enjoy being alone, even to accept my loneliness. My loneliness will never go away even though I am greatly loved, especially by my wife. Loneliness is a part of the human condition that can only be met ultimately by God. I take great comfort in Jesus' cry of dereliction: "My God, my God, why have you forsaken me?" As the words of the prayer say, "He came as one of us; he even knew our loneliness."

The more we deny our loneliness, the more we will run from ourselves and God. The strength to accept the bitter-sweet pain of loneliness is a gift from God. "Yea though I walk through the valley of the shadow of death I will fear no evil, for Thou art with me." What a promise! Let us celebrate that we are never alone, even when we are by ourselves.

check your escalator day 6

I cast myself down I know not how, under a certain fig-tree, giving full vent to my tears; and the floods of mine eyes gushed out an acceptable sacrifice to Thee. And, not indeed in these words, yet to this purpose, spake I much unto Thee: and Thou, O Lord, how long? How long, Lord, wilt Thou be angry for ever? Remember not our former iniquities, for I felt that I was held by them. I sent up these sorrowful words: How long, how long, "tomorrow, and tomorrow?" Why not now? Why not is there this hour an end to my uncleanness?

So was I speaking and weeping in the most bitter contrition of my heart, when, lo! I heard from a neighboring house a voice, as of boy or girl, I know not, chanting, and oft repeating, "Take up and read; Take up and read." Instantly, my countenance altered, I began to think most intently whether children were wont in any kind of play to sing such words: nor could I remember ever to have heard the like. So checking the torrent of my tears, I arose; interpreting it to be no other than a command from God to open the book, and read the first chapter I should find. For I had heard of Antony, that coming in during the reading of the Gospel, he received the admonition, as if what was being read was spoken to him: Go, sell all that thou hast, and give to the poor, and thou shalt have treasure in heaven, and come and follow me: and by such oracle he was forthwith converted unto Thee.

Eagerly then I returned to the place where Alypius was sitting; for there had I laid the volume of the apostle when I arose thence. I seized, opened, and in silence read that section on which my eyes first fell: Not in rioting and drunkenness, not in chambering and wantonness, not in strife and envying; but put ye on the Lord Jesus Christ, and make not provision for the flesh, in concupiscence. No further would I read; nor needed I: for instantly at the end of this sentence, by a light as it were of serenity infused into my heart, all the darkness of doubt vanished away.

Saint Augustine, The Confessions Of Saint Augustine

We are the hollow men.
We are the stuffed men.
Leaning together. Headpiece
filled with straw. Alas!
Our dried voices when we whisper
together are quiet and meaningless
As wind in dry grass or rat's feet over
broken glass in our dry cellar.
Shape without form, shade without color
Paralysed force, gesture without motion.

T.S. Eliot, The Hollow Men

But Saul, still breathing threats and murder against the disciples of the Lord, went to the high priest and asked him for letters to the synagogues at Damascus, so that if he found any belonging to the Way, men or women, he might bring them bound to Jerusalem. Now as he journeyed he approached Damascus, and suddenly a light from heaven flashed about him. And he fell to the ground and heard a voice saying to him, "Saul, Saul, why do you persecute me?" And he said, "Who are you, Lord?" And he said, "I am Jesus, whom you are persecuting; but rise and enter the city, and you will be told what to do." The men who were traveling with him stood speechless, hearing the voice but seeing no one. Saul arose from the ground; and when his eyes were opened, he could see nothing; so they led him by the hand and brought him into Damascus. And for three days he was without sight, and neither ate nor drank.

Acts 9:1-9

For this people's heart has grown dull,
and their ears are heavy of hearing,
and their eyes they have closed;
lest they should perceive with their eyes,
and hear with their ears,
and understand with their hearts,
and turn for me to heal them

Acts 28:27

day 6

The word is near you, on your lips and in your heart (that is, the word of faith which we preach); because, if you confess with your lips that Jesus is Lord and believe in your heart that God raised him from the dead, you will be saved. For man believes with his heart and so is justified, and he confesses with his lips and so is saved.

Romans 10:8-10

Now after John was arrested, Jesus came into Galilee, preaching the gospel of God, and saying, "The time is fulfilled, and the kingdom of God is at hand; repent, and believe the gospel." And passing along by the Sea of Galilee, he saw Simon and Andrew the brother of Simon casting a net in the sea; for they were fishermen. And Jesus said to them, "Follow me and I will make you become fishers of men." And immediately they left their nets and followed him. And going on a little farther, he saw James the son of Zeb'edee and John his brother, who were in their boat mending the nets. And immediately he called them; and they left their father Zeb'edee in the boat with the hired servants, and followed him

Mark 1:14-20

At that time the disciples came to Jesus, saying, "Who is the greatest in the kingdom of heaven?" And calling to him a child, he put him in the midst of them, and said, "Truly, I say to you, unless you turn and become like children, you will never enter the kingdom of heaven. Whoever humbles himself like this child, he is the greatest in the kingdom of heaven."

Matthew 18:1-4

day 6

CHECK YOUR ESCALATOR

Rachel Carson's book, *The Sea Around Us*, describes the microscopic vegetable life of the sea which provides food for many of the ocean's large and small creatures. These little plants drift thousands of miles wherever the currents carry them, with no power or will of their own to direct their destiny. They are called plankton, from a Greek word which means "wandering" or "drifting."

If plankton is an accurate term for the wandering plant life of the ocean, it may also be accurate for us. Too many people have lost their sense of direction; they feel powerless to direct their own destiny; they are without purpose in the world. T.S. Eliot's 1925 poem, "The Hollow Men," still says it well:

"Shape without form, shade without color,

Paralysed force, gesture without motion."

If it is true that we are drifting, that we lack a high calling and a sense of purpose, then it is now time to be converted.

There's a tough word—conversion. So many do not understand it or see the need of it, yet Jesus announced the beginning of his ministry with the words, "The time is fulfilled and the kingdom of God is at hand. Repent and believe in the gospel."

The Greek word for repent is *metanoia*. It means turning around—in military terms, doing a sharp, "About! Face!" The Latin word for conversion means "a turning toward" something. That seems more positive, but both a turning about and a turning toward are involved.

It's the nature of the experience that divides us. Conversion usually happens through a crisis or through a process. Call one "the earthquake experience" and the other "the escalator experience."

Each time San Francisco has remembered the anniversary of the 1906 earthquake, it is remarkable what survivors recalled. It was, however, an experience of such magnitude, a moment of such crisis, that their memories were sharp and accurate.

So it is with those who experienced conversion in such a radical way. They remember it well, vividly, dramatically, and can easily talk about it, and usually will at the drop of a hat. When, where, how, who, all the questions are answered. Some are embarrassed by such personal revelations and shy away from them.

They, like I, probably experienced conversion more through a process, like getting on an escalator. We stepped on the moving stairs when we were baptized into the church as small babies and entered on The Cradle Roll. The escalator carried us through church school and young peoples' programs. More people joined us as we married and had children. Then we brought our own children to board the escalator with us. It is our hope, of course, that the moving stairs end in heaven, from the cradle to the grave.

Such an experience of Christian nurture is wonderful, but it can be numbing. One can just ride on in ignorant bliss, lacking both noble calling and high purpose. Somewhere during that ride, we need to check the escalator. Where are we going, who are we with, what floor are we on? Are you just taking Jesus along for the ride or does his presence there make a difference?

Check your escalator! It may be going to the wrong place!

the awesome nature of freedom day 7

The Lord said to Cain, "Why are you angry, and why has your countenance fallen? If you do well, will you not be accepted? And if you do not do well, sin is crouching at the door.... Cain said to Abel his brother, "Let us go out to the field." And when they were in the field, Cain rose up against his brother Abel, and killed him.

Genesis 4:6-8

No one is handed freedom on a platter. You must make your own freedom. If someone hands it to you, it is not freedom at all, but the alms of a benefactor who will invariably ask a price of you in return.

Freedom means you are unobstructed in ruling your own life as you choose. Anything less is a form of slavery. If you cannot be unrestrained in making choices, in living as you dictate, in doing as you please with your body (provided your pleasure does not interfere with anyone else's freedom), then you are without the command I am talking about, and in essence you are being victimized.

To be free does not mean denying your responsibilities to your loved ones and your fellow man. Indeed, it includes the freedom to make choices to be responsible. But nowhere is it dictated that you must be what others want you to be when their wishes conflict with what you want for yourself. You can be responsible and free. Most of the people who will try to tell you that you cannot, who will label your push for freedom "selfish", will turn out to have measures of authority over your life, and will really be protesting your threat to the holds you have allowed them to have on you. If they can help you feel selfish, they've contributed to your feeling guilty, and immobilized you again...

The freest people in the world are those who have senses of inner peace about themselves: They simply refuse to be swayed by the whims of others, and are quietly effective at running their own lives. These people enjoy freedom from role definitions in which they must behave in certain ways because they are parents, employees, Americans, or even adults; they enjoy freedom to breathe whatever air they choose, in whatever location, without worrying about how everyone else feels about their choices. They are responsible people, but they are not enslaved by other people's selfish interpretations of what responsibility is.

Wayne W. Dyer, Pulling Your Own Strings

"Perhaps I shall come away with you," Zorba's boss said to him. "I'm free."

Zorba shook his head. "No, you're not free," he said. "The string you're tied to is perhaps longer than other people's. That's all. You're on a long piece of string, boss; you come and go, and think you're free, but you never cut the string in two. And when people don't cut the string..."

"I'll cut it some day!" I said defiantly, because Zorba's words had touched an open wound in me and hurt.

"It's difficult, boss, very difficult. You need a touch of folly to do that; folly, d'you see? You have to risk everything! But you've got such a strong head, it'll always get the better of you. A man's head is like a grocer; it keeps accounts: I've paid so much and earned so much and that means a profit of this much or a loss of that much. The head's a careful little shopkeeper; it never risks all it has, always keeps something in reserve. It never breaks the string. Ah no! ... If the string slips out of its grasp, the head, poor devil, is lost, finished! But if a man doesn't break the string, tell me, what flavor is left in life? The flavor of camomile, weak camomile tea! Nothing like rum—that makes you see life inside out!"

Nikos Kazantzakis, Zorba The Greek

day 7

Jesus then said to the Jews who had believed in him, "If you continue in my word, you are truly my disciples, and you will know the truth and the truth will set you free." They answered him, "We are descendants of Abraham, and have never been in bondage to any one. How is it that you say, 'You will be made free'?"

Jesus answered them, "Truly, truly, I say to you, every one who commits sin is a slave to sin. The slave does not continue in the house for ever; the son continues for ever. So if the Son makes you free, you will be free indeed."

John 8:31-35

And while he was at Bethany in the house of Simon the leper, as he sat at table, a woman came with an alabaster jar of ointment of pure nard, very costly, and she broke the jar and poured it over his head. But there were some who said to themselves indignantly, "Why was the ointment thus wasted? For this ointment might have sold for more than three hundred denarii, and given to the poor." And they reproached her. But Jesus said, "Let her alone; why do you trouble her? She has done a beautiful thing to me. For you always have the poor with you, and whenever you will, you can do good to them; but you will not always have me. She has done what she could; she has anointed my body beforehand for burying. And truly, I say to you, wherever the gospel is preached in the whole world, what she has done will be told in memory of her."

Mark 14:3-9

What fears or other "strings" are restricting your freedom? Are you exercising your freedom in a way that takes seriously its potentially awesome consequences?

day 7

THE AWESOME NATURE OF FREEDOM

The awesome nature of freedom struck me hardest years ago when I was asked to officiate at the funeral of two young boys killed on a motorcycle while trying to escape the police. Agony, grief, and woe were evident throughout our community. Hundreds of young people attended the service. What to say? Why did God let this happen?

John Steinbeck's writing helped. "We may conquer sin or we may not." We are truly free to create or destroy. God did not send those young men to a party and force them to drink nor did God place them on a motorcycle and tell them to avoid the police. The awesome nature of freedom is that we can destroy ourselves.

Recently the San Francisco Bay Area suffered a terribly destructive earthquake. Statements were being made about the judgment of God on "Sin City." If two and a half million people choose to live in an area where faults abound, why is that God's judgment? Anyone in The Bay Area is free to move, but we choose to stay and live with both real and potential disaster, knowing full well those continental plates may shift at any time.

America is a land of freedoms—in principle, freedom from want, fear, hunger; freedom of speech, religion, and the press. It all sounds good. Most of us celebrate our freedoms. Like the Pharisees who claimed to be free because of their heritage, we, too, claim to be free because of our heritage.

Yet no one is handed freedom on a platter. As an ad for a stock brokerage firm once said, "You have to earn it." But we don't truly believe that; we expect to be free to do whatever we please whenever we want to do it. And when it doesn't work out that way we claim to be victims, victims of circumstances, victims of ill-intentioned people, victims of fate. Sometimes we really are victims. But sometimes the truth is that we are victims of our own irresponsible attitudes.

Jesus speaks to us as he did to those Pharisees, "You shall know the truth and the truth shall set you free." The implication seems to be that a relationship with God through that same Jesus will enable any one of us to see things differently and to know the truth about life, about ourselves.

Most of us don't want to find out. We'd rather be victims and put the blame on God or our neighbor or our government or... the list is endless. Blame someone and then sue them.

Zorba, the Greek has a different approach to life, one that challenges our piety—you have to cut that string and take some risks, you have to dare to be different. Being different for the sake of being different is, however, only a worse form of conformity.

We celebrate freedom but most of us aren't truly free. We chicken out at the last moment, because we can't cut the string to all our securities and we don't really want to be responsible.

Freedom is demanding and awesome. We are free to create or destroy, to love or hate, to be responsible or irresponsible, to choose our attitude about life in all circumstances, to choose whether we will commit our lives to Christ.

"You shall know the truth and the truth shall set you free." AWESOME!

believing impossible things **day 8**

"Only it is so very lonely here!" Alice said in a melancholy voice; and at the thought of her loneliness two large tears came rolling down her cheeks.

"Oh, don't go on like that!" cried the poor Queen, wringing her hands in despair. "Consider what a great girl you are. Consider what a long way you've come today. Consider what o'clock it is. Consider anything, only don't cry."

Alice could not help laughing at this, even in the midst of her tears. "Can you keep from crying by considering things?" she asked.

"That's the way it's done," the Queen said with great decision. "Nobody can do two things at once, you know. Let's consider your age, to begin with—how old are you?"

"I'm seven and a half, exactly."

"You needn't say 'exactly'," the Queen remarked; "I can believe it without that. Now I'll give you something to believe. I'm just one hundred and one, five months, and a day."

"I can't believe that!" said Alice.

"Can't you?" the Queen said in a pitying tone. "Try again; draw a long breath, and shut your eyes."

Alice laughed. "There's no use trying," she said; "one can't believe impossible things."

"I dare say you haven't had much practice," said the Queen. "When I was your age I always did it for half an hour a day. Why, sometimes I've believed as many as six impossible things before breakfast."

Lewis Carroll, Alice In Wonderland

This book would say to the modern layman, "Don't exclude yourself from the fellowship of Christ's followers because of mental difficulties. If you love Christ and are seeking to follow him, take an attitude of Christian agnosticism to intellectual problems at least for the present. Read this book to see if the essentials of the Christian religion are clarified for you and only accept those things which gradually seem to you to be true. Leave the rest in a box labeled, 'awaiting further light.' In the meantime, join with us in trying to show and spread Christ's spirit, for this, we feel, is the most important thing in the world.

Leslie D. Weatherhead, The Christian Agnostic

The Son of God, the second Person in the Trinity, being very and eternal God, of one substance, and equal with the Father, did, when the fullness of time was come, take upon him man's nature, with all the essential properties and common infirmities thereof; yet without sin: being conceived by the power of the Holy Ghost, in the womb of the Virgin Mary, of her substance. So that two whole, perfect, and distinct natures, the Godhead and the manhood, were inseparably joined together in one person, without conversion, composition, or confusion. Which person is very God and very man, yet one Christ, the only Mediator between God and man.

Westminster Confession, Chapter VIII

He has delivered us from the dominion of darkness and transferred us to the kingdom of his beloved Son, in whom we have redemption, the forgiveness of sins.

He is the image of the invisible God, the first-born of all creation; for in him all things were created, in heaven and on earth, visible and invisible, whether thrones or dominions or principalities or authorities—all things were created through him and for him. He is before all things, and in him all things hold together. He is the head of the body, the church; he is the beginning, the first-born from the dead, that in everything he might be pre-eminent. For in him all the fulness of God was pleased to dwell, and through him to reconcile to himself all things, whether on earth or in heaven, making peace by the blood of his cross.

Colossians 1:13-20

day 8

Are some religious ideas impossible for you to believe? What would it mean to have faith, even if you can't believe those ideas? Can ideas that aren't literally true be true in some other sense?

day 8

BELIEVING IMPOSSIBLE THINGS

When I read the passage from Alice in Wonderland, I am very ambivalent because I can identify with both Alice and the Queen. There are times when confronted with a particular tenet of faith that I will say with Alice (and Bishop John A. T. Robinson and other famous skeptics), "I can't believe that." But at other times I want to say with the Queen, "Why not? I practice believing impossible things!"

John Cardinal Henry Newman once said that faith is more than simple assent to a given set of propositions. Faith involves the person in commitment to an idea, or, in the case of Christianity, to a Person. Faith at its best has both its emotional as well as its cognitive side. The mind and the heart must be integrated even when full understanding is impossible. And full understanding is impossible; we are not God.

The Westminster Confession is one of the greatest creedal statements ever written; the language is one of a kind. The statement about Jesus has always attracted me and confounded me: "two whole, perfect, and distinct natures, the Godhead and the manhood, were inseparably joined together in one person, without conversion, composition or confusion."

Reading that arouses my ambivalence again. What are they talking about? "I can't believe that!" Yet I have practiced "believing impossible things." Perhaps a clue to the riddle lies in acknowledging that I cannot grasp what in the world they are describing, but in my heart I know they are right. I believe about Jesus what they were attempting to say.

On the one hand, I have no idea what they are talking about—the exact description of how Jesus was God. On the other hand, I know what they have experienced and how hard it is to put it into words. Isn't it that way an awful lot of the time? How does one describe the indescribable? Jokingly we say, "How does one unscrew the inscrutable?"

Paul says in Colossians, "He is the image of the invisible God, the first-born of all creation; for in him all things were created, in heaven and on earth, visible and invisible, whether thrones or dominions or principalities or authorities—all things were created through him and for him. He is before all things and in him all things hold together."

I feel like saying with Alice, "I can't believe that!" Yet the Queen and I have been practicing believing impossible things. The reality Paul struggles with is one I struggle with too, and I claim that Christ for my own.

I like being a "Christian Agnostic," as long as I don't have to give up "believing impossible things." If that seems contradictory, then so be it. At the heart of life is a great mystery and we don't always serve God well when we try to act as though we have the only key to the mystery. Sometimes it is better to be caught between not-believing and believing, between Alice and the Queen. Sometimes it is better to confess our ignorance, our agnosticism, our amazement. Then, like the father of the child whom Jesus healed, we cry out, "Lord, I believe; help, Thou, mine unbelief."

some people are more equal than others **day 9**

And a moment later, out from the door of the farmhouse came a long file of pigs, all walking on their hind legs. Some did it better than others, one or two were even a trifle unsteady and looked as though they would have the support of a stick, but every one of them made his way right round the yard successfully. And finally there was a tremendous baying of dogs and a shrill crowing from the black cockerel, and out came Napoleon himself, majestically upright, casting haughty glances from side to side, and with his dogs gambolling round him.

He carried a whip in his trotter.

There was a deadly silence. Amazed, terrified, huddling together, the animals watched the long line of pigs march slowly round the yard. It was as though the world had turned upside-down.

Then there came a moment when the first shock had worn off and when, in spite of everything—in spite of their terror of the dogs, and of the habit, developed through long years, of never complaining, never criticizing, no matter what happened—they might have uttered some word of protest. But just at that moment, as though at a signal, all the sheep burst out into a tremendous bleating of—"Four legs good, two legs better! Four legs good, two legs betters! Four legs good, two legs better!"

It went on for five minutes without stopping. And by the time the sheep had quieted down, the chance to utter any protest had passed, for the pigs had marched back into the farmhouse.

Benjamin felt a nose nuzzling at his shoulder. He looked around. It was Clover. Her old eyes looked dimmer than ever. Without saying anything, she tugged gently at his mane and led him round to the end of the big barn, where the Seven Commandments were written. For a minute or two they stood gazing at the tarred wall with its white lettering.

"My sight is failing," she said finally. "Even when I was young I could not have read what was written there. But it appears to me that that wall locks different. Are the Seven Commandments the same as they used to be, Benjamin?"

For once Benjamin consented to break his rule, and he read out to her what was written on the wall. There was nothing now except a single Commandment. It ran:
ALL ANIMALS ARE EQUAL
BUT SOME ANIMALS ARE MORE
EQUAL THAN OTHERS

George Orwell, Animal Farm

We hold these Truths to be self-evident, that all Men are created equal, that they are endowed by their Creator with certain unalienable Rights, that among these are Life, Liberty, and the Pursuit of Happiness.

The Declaration of Independence

You shall know the truth and the truth shall set you free.

John 8:32

By this we know that we abide in him and he in us, because he has given us of his own Spirit. And we have seen and testify that the Father has sent his Son as the Savior of the world. Whoever confesses that Jesus is the Son of God, God abides in him, and he in God. So we know and believe the love God has for us. God is love, and he who abides in love abides in God, and God abides in him. In this is love perfected with us, that we may have confidence for the day of judgment, because as he is so are we in this world. There is no fear in love, but perfect love casts out fear. For fear has to do with punishment, and he who fears is not perfected in love. We love, because he first loved us. If any one says, "I love God," and hates his brother, he is a liar; for he who does not love his brother whom he has seen, cannot love God whom he has not seen. And this commandment we have from him, that he who loves God should love his brother also.

I John 4:13-21

day 9

What kinds of inequality do you encounter in your daily life? How can you make a practical difference to help bring greater equality to people oppressed by injustice?

day 9

SOME PEOPLE ARE MORE EQUAL THAN OTHERS

I get goose bumps every time I read Dr. Martin Luther King Jr.'s "I Have a Dream" speech. It is one of the great speeches of history, yet all kinds of White Americans—whether religious or not—refuse to hear the power of the words. They dismiss King by saying things like, "Martin Luther King does not deserve a holiday in his name. He was a rabble-rousing, Communist-inspired, over-sexed Black man. Nothing more!"

For me, King was one of the great men of this century, if not all centuries. For many people, both Black and White, King was a latter-day Moses: a visionary who perceived a promised land of racial justice amidst suffocating racial oppression, and a leader who was willing to sacrifice everything to bring his people to that promised land.

Those who want to dismiss King often emphasize the public scandals surrounding him. But one can be a great visionary and leader while having real character flaws. In recent times we have found out far more about the sex lives of American Presidents than we ever wanted to know, and it's not a pretty picture! Maybe we should heed the words of the Psalmist, "If thou, Lord, shouldst mark iniquities, O Lord, who shall stand?"

I suspect the real problem provoking King's detractors is that a Black man could lead his people so far and challenge White authority so much. Prejudice runs deep in America! We like to blame it on the Deep South, but prejudice knows no bounds. Prejudice runs just as deeply in The San Francisco Bay Area as it does in The Mississippi Bayou. In the South the percentage of Black people is much higher and the population more concentrated so the awareness of racial differences is intensified. Tolerance usually grows in direct proportion to distance from the problem.

California's problem is different—it involves Laotians, Cambodians, Koreans, Filipinos, Chinese, Japanese, Hispanics, and the beat goes on. Orwell's awful truth describes our situation all too well—"all people are equal, but some people are more equal than others." All the pious protestations in the world won't change that.

Facing the truth is painful but it is the only thing that works in the long run. All human beings are prejudiced, including the above-named racial groups and the White people who interact with them. It takes a constant reexamination of prejudices to change. That's why change is so slow and at times nonexistent. It takes too much effort and it hurts too much.

As the song says, "We have been carefully taught" and we will not surrender our prejudices easily. Those in power will use every sleight-of-hand trick and every type of rhetoric to convince us that they are not prejudiced. They want us to believe they are open-minded and working solely for the common good. Ho! Ho! Ho! Merry Christmas!

It will take a lot of repentance (on everyone's part) and a lot of grace before real integration and racial justice becomes a reality in our land. Whether we are willing to pay the price remains to be seen. We were willing to pay for putting a man on the moon and exploring the planets, but are we willing to pay the necessary price in sweat, blood, and tears, as well as money, to see that we can live in harmony with one another on earth?

"If anyone says, 'I love God,' and hates his brother, he is a liar." As long as "some people are more equal than others," we are all liars. Let freedom ring!

the lusts that drive us day 10

Some people say there is no such thing as progress. The fact that human beings are now the only animals left on Earth, I confess, seems a confusing sort of victory. Those of you familiar with the nature of my earlier published works will understand why I mourned especially when the last beaver died.

There were two monsters sharing this planet with us when I was a boy, however, and I celebrate their extinction today. They were determined to kill us, or at least make our lives meaningless. They came close to success. They were cruel adversaries, which my little friends the beavers were not. Lions? No. Tigers? No. Lions and tigers snoozed most of the time. The monsters I will name never snoozed. They inhabited our heads. They were the arbitrary lusts for gold, and, God help us, for a glimpse of a little girl's underpants.

I thank those lusts for being so ridiculous, for they taught us that it was possible for a human being to believe anything, and to behave passionately in keeping with that belief—any belief.

So now we can build an unselfish society by devoting to unselfishness the frenzy we once devoted to gold and to underpants.

Kurt Vonnegut, Breakfast Of Champions

Countess: Tell me the reason why wilt thou marry.
Clown: My poor body, madam, requires it; I am driven on by the flesh, and he must needs go that the devil drives.
Shakespeare, All's Well that Ends Well

When the unclean spirit has gone out of a man, he passes through waterless places seeking rest, but he finds none. Then he says, "I will return to my house from which I came." And when he comes he finds it empty, swept, and put in order. Then he goes and brings with him seven other spirits more evil than himself, and they enter and dwell there; and the last state of that man becomes worse than the first. So shall it be also with this evil generation.

Matthew 12:43-45

So I gave them up to their own heart's lust:
And they walked in their own counsels.

Psalm 81:12 (KJV)

Lust not after her beauty in thine heart;
Neither let her take thee with her eyelids.

Proverbs 6:25 (KJV)

This I say then: Walk in the Spirit, and you shall not fulfill the lust of the flesh. For the flesh lusts against the Spirit, and the Spirit against the flesh; and these are contrary to one another, so that you do not do the things you wish.

Galatians 5:16-17 (NKJV)

For all that is in the world—the lust of the flesh, the lust of the eyes, and the pride of life—is not of the Father but is of the world. And the world is passing away, and the lust of it; but he who does the will of God abides forever.

I John 2:16-17 (NKJV)

And Peter, fastening his eyes upon the lame man with John, said, Look on us. And he gave heed to them, expecting to receive something of them. Then Peter said, "Silver and gold have I none; but such as I have give I thee: In the name of Jesus of Nazareth rise and walk."

Acts 3:4-6

day 10

Does lust for sex, money, or power sometimes consume you, drawing your attention away from higher and more noble purposes? How would your life be different if you could tame these out-of-control desires? What goals and purposes would you like to pursue instead?

day 10

THE LUSTS THAT DRIVE US

I see England,
I see France;
I see someone's
Underpants.

Hearing the recitation of that playground ditty used to embarrass me a great deal as a little boy. No one had talked to me about sex and I was slow in understanding. Little did I realize that such an interest in sex among little boys would grow and grow until one day I heard a grown man say, "If you're not thinking about sex all the time, you've lost your concentration."

Camaraderie among men, without women, can be very enjoyable. It can also be depressing, however, to see the depths to which men can sink in their joking about and lusting after women. Too many men, despite having a lovely wife and family at home, are somehow able to bifurcate their minds so that chasing other women remains separate and unrelated. Lust overcomes any inhibitions or prohibitions. If God intended our interest in sex to be so strong that we would indeed reproduce, well, it was a success. Our culture inundates us with sexual images, innuendo, and double entendre. "Underpants" are everywhere, literally and figuratively.

Only the lust for gold can match the lust for sex. The two are closely related for money easily buys sex, in both raw and sophisticated forms. The man who has both money and women is too often secretly, if not openly, envied. Men love to display the accoutrements of their success—clothes, cars, airplanes, and women all become symbols of achievement. A modern bumper sticker voices a popular belief: "In the end the man with the most toys wins."

People with lots of money are hard to reach; they tend to be preoccupied with what they have; they often become insensitive to others. Since they can buy their way out of most difficulties, they credit themselves with greater abilities than they actually possess. No wonder Jesus said, "It is harder for a rich man to get into the kingdom of heaven than it is for a camel to go through the eye of a needle."

Lust is defined as "intense desire or need, craving." It is disheartening to think of how much of the world is caught up in its two favorite lusts—"underpants and gold." And lusting it is—intense desire and craving for pleasure and happiness. So intense is the desire that it blocks all awareness of the swiftly passing days and the ephemeral nature of such pleasure.

The little New Testament book of 1st John says it best, "For all that is in the world—the lust of the flesh, the lust of the eyes, and the pride of life—is not of the Father but is of the world. And the world is passing away, and the lust of it; but he who does the will of God abides forever."

All the gold in the world will not buy more time and all the sex in the world will not bring more satisfaction. Unfortunately, we are "too soon old, too late smart."

different strokes for different folks day 11

Our age is retrospective. It builds the sepulchres of the fathers. It writes biographies, histories, and criticism. The foregoing generations beheld God and nature face to face; we, through their eyes. Why should not we also enjoy an original relation to the universe? Why should not we have a poetry and philosophy of insight and not of tradition, and a religion by revelation to us, and not the history of theirs? Embosomed for a season in nature, whose floods of life stream around and through us, and invite us by the powers they supply, to action proportioned to nature, why should we grope among the dry bones of the past, or put the living generation into masquerade out of its faded wardrobe? The sun shines today also. There is more wool and flax in the fields. There are new lands, new men, new thoughts. Let us demand our own works and laws and worship.

Ralph Waldo Emerson, Nature

Ought it to be assumed that in all men the mixture of religion with other elements should be identical? Ought it, indeed, to be assumed that the lives of all men should show identical religious elements? In other words, is the existence of so many religious types and sects and creeds regrettable?

To the questions I answer "NO" emphatically. And my reason is that I do not see how it is possible that creatures in such different positions and with such different powers as human beings are, should have exactly the same functions and the same duties. No two of us have identical difficulties, nor should we work out identical solutions. Each, from his peculiar angle of observations, takes in a certain sphere of fact and trouble, which each must deal with in a unique manner. One of us must soften himself, another must harden himself; one must yield a point, another must stand firm—in order the better to defend the position assigned him. If an Emerson were forced to be a Wesley, or a Moody forced to be a Whitman, the total human consciousness of the divine would suffer. The divine can mean no single quality, it must mean a group of qualities, by being champions of which in alternation, different men may all find worthy missions. Each attitude being a syllable in human nature's total message, it takes the whole of us to spell the meaning out completely. So a "god of battles" must be allowed to be the god for one kind of a person, a "god of peace and heaven and home," the god for another. We must frankly recognize the fact that we live in partial systems, and that parts are not interchangeable in the spiritual life. If we are peevish and jealous, destruction of the self must be an element of our religions; why need it be one if we are good and sympathetic from the outset? If we are sick souls, we require a religion of deliverance; but why think so much of deliverance? Unquestionably, some men have the completer experience and the higher vocation, here just as in the social world; but for each man to stay in his own experience, whate'er it be, and for others to tolerate him there, is surely best.

William James, The Varieties Of Religious Experience

Great is the Lord, and greatly to be praised,
and his greatness is unsearchable.

Psalm 145:3

Behold, God is great, and we know him not;
the number of his years is unsearchable.

Job 36:26

God thunders wondrously with his voice;
He does great things which we
cannot comprehend.

Job 37:5

Can you find out the deep things of God?
Can you find out the limit of the Almighty?
It is higher than heaven--what can you do?
Deeper than Sheol--what can you know?

day 11

Job 11:7, 8

For affliction does not come from the dust,
nor does trouble sprout from the ground;
But man is born to trouble
as the sparks fly upward.
As for me, I would seek God,
and to God would I commit my cause;
Who does great things and unsearchable,
marvelous things without number.

Job 5:6-9

So Paul, standing in the middle of the Areopagas, said: "Men of Athens, I perceive that in every way you are very religious. For as I passed along, and observed the objects of your worship, I found also an altar with this inscription, 'To an unknown God.' What therefore you worship as unknown, this I proclaim to you. The God who made the world and everything in it, being Lord of heaven and earth, does not live in shrines made by man, nor is he served by human hands, as though he had need of anything, since he himself gives to all men life and breath and everything. And he made from one every nation of men to live on all the face of the earth, having determined allotted periods and the boundaries of their habitation, that they should seek God, in the hope that they might feel after him and find him. Yet he is not far from each one of us, for 'In him we live and move and have our being;' as even some of your poets have said, 'For we are indeed his offspring.'

Being then God's offspring, we ought not to think that the Deity is like gold, or silver, or stone, a representation by the art and imagination of man. The times of ignorance God overlooked, but now he commands all men everywhere to repent, because he has fixed a day on which he will judge the world in righteousness by a man whom he has appointed, and of this he has given assurance to all men by raising him from the dead."

Now when they heard of the resurrection of the dead, some mocked; but others said, "We will hear you again about this."

Acts 17:22-32

How do your beliefs differ from what you've been told you're "supposed" to believe? How do you make sense of the enormous diversity of people's religious beliefs? Do you think there is one true answer to religious questions? Or are there many different religious truths?

day 11

DIFFERENT STROKES FOR DIFFERENT FOLKS

It was in that different and difficult decade of the sixties that the rock group, Earth, Wind and Fire first sang a song with the words, "Different strokes for different folks." Those words were to prove prophetic, for it was a time in which being different was "in." Variety was, indeed, the spice of life. What was true for social intercourse became equally true for theology and religion. Pluralism became the order of the day and "new age awareness" brought a multiplicity of choices for religious folks.

The history of dogma shows that "there is nothing new under the sun," but it is perhaps safe to say that never has there been a time when so many different people believed so many different things. Institutional religion with its dogma lost its appeal (except for very conservative people); people tuned out the church and the synagogue and the temple and tuned in to themselves and their own thoughts and feelings.

William James writing in the early part of the century told us that people are very different and, therefore, need different forms of religion. We didn't want to believe him and dismissed him as "just another psychologist."

Decades in the ministry of the church have convinced me. People are different, unique, strange, even a little weird. They will believe what they jolly well want to believe, and no preacher, evangelist, bishop, or pope will make them believe otherwise. They may affirm the acceptable dogma in public, but when they are questioned privately, it is truly "different strokes for different folks."

Many times I have taken a group of church people, some considered the "pillars of the church," and asked them to tell me, "What do you think happens at the moment you die?" When pinned down, some of these so-called "pillars" will affirm classic positions of immortality and resurrection, others accept reincarnation or the transmigration of souls, and a surprising number indicate that "when you're dead, you're dead." That's it. Kaput! Nothing more.

For a long while, I was aghast. I couldn't believe what they didn't believe. Now I know that's the way it is. Our images of sweet, soft-spoken grandmothers at whose knees we can sit and learn the Bible and what we should believe about God are delusions. Those grandmothers may be sweet and soft-spoken and know the Bible well and have impeccable character, but only God knows what they really believe. And all the church councils and proclamations of dogma and threats of hellfire and protestations of important people aren't going to change that.

I rather like that. At the heart of life is a great mystery and at times the less said about it, the better. At other times it is important for us to affirm what we do believe: "I believe in Jesus Christ as my Lord and Savior." Or better yet to sing, "Amazing grace, how sweet the sound, that saved a wretch like me. I once was lost, but now I'm found, was blind but now I see."

"Great is the Lord, and greatly to be praised, and his greatness is unsearchable."

The truth is that it has been, now is, and always will be: "Different strokes for different folks."

crap-detecting day 12

Who knows himself a braggart,
Let him fear this; for it will come to pass
That every braggart shall be found an ass.
Rust sword, cool blushes, and, Parolles, live
Safest in shame! Being fool'd, by fool'ry thrive!
There's place and means for every man alive.

William Shakespeare, All's Well That Ends Well

You can't put sawdust
in a meat pie
and expect it to be tasty.

Roy Miles

The heart is deceitful above all things and desperately corrupt; who can understand it? "I the LORD search the mind and try the heart, to give every man according to his ways, according to the fruit of his doings."

Jeremiah 17:9-10

For the word of God is living and active, sharper than any two-edged sword, piercing to the division of soul and spirit, of joints and marrow, and discerning the thoughts and intentions of the heart. And before him no creature is hidden, but all are open and laid bare to the eyes of him with whom we have to do.

Hebrews 4:12-13

Beware of practicing your piety before men in order to be seen by them; for then you will have no reward from your Father who is in heaven.

Thus, when you give alms, sound no trumpet before you, as the hypocrites do in the synagogues and in the streets, that they may be praised by men. Truly, I say to you, they have received their reward. But when you give alms, do not let your left hand know what your right hand is doing, so that your alms may be in secret; and your Father who sees in secret will reward you.

And when you pray, you must not be like the hypocrites; for they love to stand and pray in the synagogues and at the street corners, that they may be seen by men. Truly, I say to you, they have received their reward. But when you pray, go into your room and shut the door and pray to your Father who is in secret; and your Father who sees in secret will reward you.

Matthew 6:1-6

Beware of the leaven of the Pharisees, which is hypocrisy. Nothing is covered up that will not be revealed, or hidden that will not be known. Therefore whatever you have said in the dark shall be heard in the light, and what you have whispered in private rooms shall be proclaimed upon the housetops.

Luke 12:1-3

And his gifts were that some should be apostles, some prophets, some evangelists, some pastors and teachers, for the equipment of the saints, for the work of ministry, for building up the body of Christ, until we all attain to the unity of the faith and of the knowledge of the Son of God, to mature manhood, to the measure of the stature of the fullness of Christ; so that we may no longer be children, tossed to and fro and carried about with every wind of doctrine, by the cunning of men, by their craftiness in deceitful wiles. Rather, speaking the truth in love, we are to grow up in every way into him who is the head, into Christ, from which the whole body, joined and knit together by every joint with which it is supplied, when each part is working properly, makes bodily growth and upbuilds itself in love.

Ephesians 4:11-16

Beloved, do not believe every spirit, but test the spirits to see whether they are of God; for many false prophets have gone out into the world. By this you know the Spirit of God: every spirit which confesses that Jesus Christ has come in the flesh is of God, and every spirit which does not confess Jesus is not of God.

1 John 4:1-2

day 12

How well is your personal crap-detector working? Are there areas of your life where you're not being honest with your loved ones or with yourself? What difference would it make if you lived in the belief that every secret of the heart is known to God and that everything hidden will one day be made known?

day 12

CRAP-DETECTING

"The world is full of it," so goes the saying. It is certainly full of rhetoric, grandiloquent words spoken from every conceivable posture—women's liberation; gay and lesbian rights; civil rights for Blacks, Indian Americans, Hispanics, and Filipinos; assertion of White identity; the Right to Life Movement and the Pro-Choice Movement; ecological and environmental groups; to name only a few. At times it seems as if the whole world is posturing and we are inundated in words, words, words. Rhetoric abounds! The world is full of it!

Our world is also a world of advertising—images and more words, full of exaggeration, stretching the point, manipulation, gross distortion, and at times, outright lies. The search for truth and accuracy has never been more difficult.

It was none other than the great writer himself, Ernest Hemmingway, who, when asked what it takes to be a good writer, replied, "...a built-in, shock-proof shit detector." Indeed! To be good at anything requires a crap detector today!

The struggle to wade through all the crap that surrounds us is difficult and requires enormous energy. The necessary sharpness of mind and clarity of vision are not easy to come by. The goal of a first-class college education should be "a built-in, shock-proof shit detector." Indelicate language, profound truth!

Crap-detecting begins with the self. We, like the world, are "full of it." If we cannot be honest enough to detect in our own favorite speeches some amount of "transcendent bullshit," the chances are that we will never detect it in others. Being an idealist, a true-believer, an advocate of the right way (whatever that way may be) makes one very susceptible, because if we can easily convince ourselves of our "truth," others will all too easily convince us of their "truth."

Unhappily, the church, too, is "full of it" and doesn't have enough people with good crap detectors. Pulpiteers are no exception and those who quote the most scripture are often the worst offenders. Since we are sinners, there will always be a gap between the words we speak and the actions we take, but a good crap detector will close the gap considerably.

I once said to a congregation at the announcement period, "Anyone who hasn't broken their New Year's resolutions, stand up." No one stood. A woman, who at that moment was emotionally disturbed, misunderstood the question and the response; she thought the congregation was being hypocritical. She stood up, came forward, proceeded to the pulpit, and to everyone's horror, grabbed the microphone and shouted, "Bullshit!" She then went back and sat down.

I suspect that we have all wanted to stand before an assembled crowd and say, "Bullshit!" Decorum and lack of courage prevent us, or perhaps, the lack of a good crap detector. The lady may have misunderstood in her upset emotional state, but her crap detector was working just fine.

I do not recommend that Christians disrupt worship services by shouting obscenities, but I do recommend that we use the Bible (the world's greatest crap-detector) to examine the values of this world so "full of it," and speak the truth to one another in love.

a simple notion of being good day 13

Though the cause of evil prosper,
yet the truth alone is strong;
Though her portion be the scaffold,
and upon the throne be wrong,
Yet that scaffold sways the future,
and, behind the dim unknown,
Standeth God within the shadow
keeping watch above his own.

James Russell Lowell

While we were yet helpless, at the right time Christ died for the ungodly. Why, one will hardly die for a righteous man—though perhaps for a good man one will dare even to die. But God shows his love for us in that while we were yet sinners Christ died for us.

Romans 5:6-8

Unlike the unhurried and even life of the Amish, I did want to go overboard, be consumed by a project, and at times lose all sense of proportion. Maybe I needed to give myself totally to something, to feel the ache that goes along with the joy, to realize how much I have to give up when I'm being single-minded. What I carry in my heart is an awareness of the values intrinsic to their way of life, something to aim for.

Finding a balance I can live with—that's what I was after. The proportions need constant attention and readjusting. How much red, blue, and yellow do I need, both in my art and in my life?

* * * * *

I had been afraid to tell friends what touched me most deeply, because it might sound simplistic, corny, banal. On one of those days when I was feeling particularly miserable, a friend told me about her six-year-old grandson who was helping his father puzzle out how to mend a broken lamp while his grandfather looked on.

"Do you know how talented your father is at fixing things?" the proud grandfather asked.

"Yes," the boy said with a serious expression on his face, "but do you know what he's really best at?"

"What?" the surprised grandfather asked.

"He's best at loving."

Is loving banal?

I went back to the dictionary and looked up banal. The first definitions were "trite" and "insipid." I knew that. But then I read on and found "commonness." Maybe the things we share in common are the most important things.

Is loving simple?

Listening to your heart is not simple. Finding out who you are is not simple. It takes a lot of hard work and courage to get to know who you are and what you want.

Sue Bender, Plain And Simple

At that time the disciples came to Jesus saying, "Who is the greatest in the kingdom of heaven?" And calling to him a child, he put him in the midst of them, and said, "Truly, I say to you, unless you turn and become like little children, you will never enter the kingdom of heaven. Whoever humbles himself like this child, he is the greatest n the kingdom of heaven. Whoever receives one such child in my name receives me; but whoever causes one of these little ones who believe in me to sin, it would be better for him to have a great millstone fastened round his neck and to be drowned in the depth of the sea. See that you do not despise one of these little ones; for I tell you that in heaven their angels always behold the face of my Father who is in heaven."

Matthew 18:1-6, 10

Then children were brought to him that he might lay his hands on them and pray. The disciples rebuked the people; but Jesus said, "Let the children come to me, and do not hinder them; for to such belongs the kingdom of heaven." And he laid his hands on them and went away.

Matthew 19:13-15

day 13

When the Son of Man comes in his glory, and all the angels with him, then he will sit on the throne of his glory. All the nations will be gathered before him, and he will separate people one from another as a shepherd separates the sheep from the goats, and he will put the sheep at his right hand and the goats at the left. Then the king will say to those at his right hand, 'Come, you that are blessed by my Father, inherit the kingdom prepared for you from the foundation of the world; for I was hungry and you gave me food, I was thirsty and you gave me something to drink, I was a stranger and you welcomed me, I was naked and you gave me clothing, I was sick and you took care of me, I was in prison and you visited me.' Then the righteous will answer him, 'Lord, when was it that we saw you hungry and gave you food, or thirsty and gave you something to drink? And when was it that we saw you a stranger and welcomed you, or naked and gave you clothing? And when was it that we saw you sick or in prison and visited you?' And the king will answer them, 'Truly I tell you, just as you did it to one of the least of these who are members of my family, you did it to me.'

Matthew 25:31-40

day 13

A SIMPLE NOTION OF BEING GOOD

It is amazing how a simple idea catches on. J. D. Salinger's novel, *The Catcher in the Rye* has been fought over now for several generations. Even today the language and behavior of teenagers found in the book causes some parents to want it stricken from the list of books to be read by high school students. For others of us the book hardly seems a *cause célèbre*.

A simple idea from Salinger's story caught on and stays with us—the catcher in the rye. The novel's character Holden Caulfield had a powerful desire to protect little children, to be ready to catch them if necessary. It's a wonderful notion. Why has it captivated so many readers?

The catcher in the rye reminds me of God's love: "standeth God within the shadow keeping watch above his own." We recall the special place that children have in the teachings of Jesus—"Whoever receives one such child in my name receives me...See that you do not despise one of these little ones."

Perhaps that simple idea is important in yet a different manner. It opens up the possibility of serving God in a simple way—"catching children," watching over them. Too many of us have grandiose notions of saving the world for Christ. We have great dreams and elaborate schemes of how to save the world, or at least our part of it. We get caught up in our favorite causes. Our advocacy is crucial to the world's survival.

We need to remind ourselves that we can serve God in very simple ways. Obviously, there is nothing new about such an idea, but in a sophisticated, technological world we quickly pass beyond the obvious and simple. That we can serve God by simply being a good neighbor, by loving others, by doing humble things, by giving "a cup of cold water in His name," is often overlooked.

As we get older such simplicity is a rather comforting notion. We don't have as much energy and desire to be the center of dramatic schemes to save people and change the world. It is reassuring to think that we can serve God just as well by "catching children" and "being kind to animals"—an exaggeration and a caricature, to be sure, but not by much.

Odds are that the grace of God is found more often in people's simple and gracious acts on behalf of one another than in larger, more dramatic ways. Mother Teresa wasn't famous when she started. Her commitment to working with the poor on a one-to-one basis brought fame, not her effort to save all the poor of the world. Fame enabled her to help far more than she ever dreamed, but it all began with her simple attempt to do and be good.

I have often wondered what to say at funeral services for people who are not church members and have never professed their faith. The best that can be said by their loved ones is, "he was a good man; he did good things for people" or "she was a fine woman; she cared for everyone around her." That's certainly better than the opposite; doing good things is acceptable to God, the judge.

Some Christians are uncomfortable with anything that smacks of salvation by works, but we also cannot deny that simple works are a more wonderful expression of the love of God than profound statements of faith. The demand for orthodoxy overlooks a very gracious text from 1st John: "Where love is, there is God."

no man is an island **day 14**

No man is an island, entire of itself;
Every man is a piece of the
continent, a part of the main;
If a clod be washed away by the
sea, Europe is the less,
As well as if a promontory were, as well as if
a manor of thy friends or of thine own were;
Any man's death diminishes me,
because I am involved in mankind;
And therefore never send to know
for whom the bell tolls;
It tolls for thee.

John Donne

There is a destiny that
makes us brothers.
No one goes his way alone.
All that we put into
the lives of others,
Comes back into our own.

Edwin Markham

For to be a woman is to have interests and duties, raying out in all directions from the central mother-core, like spokes from the hub of a wheel. The pattern of our lives is essentially circular. We must be open to all points of the compass; husband, children, friends, home, community; stretched out, exposed, sensitive like a spider's web to each breeze that blows, to each call that comes. How difficult for us, then, to achieve a balance in the midst of these contradictory tensions, and yet how necessary for the proper functioning of our lives... With a new awareness, both painful and humorous, I begin to understand why the saints were rarely married women...

What is the answer? There is no easy answer, no complete answer. I have only clues, shells from the sea. The bare beauty of the channelled whelk tells me that one answer, and perhaps a first step, is in simplification of life, in cutting out some of the distractions. But how? Total retirement is not possible. I cannot shed my responsibilities. I cannot permanently inhabit a desert island. I cannot be a nun in the midst of family life. I would not want to be. The solution for me, surely, is neither in total renunciation of the world, nor in acceptance of it. I must find a balance somewhere, or an alternating rhythm between these two extremes; a swinging of the pendulum between solitude and community, between retreat and return. In my periods of retreat, perhaps I can learn something to carry back into my worldly life.

Anne Morrow Lindbergh, Gift From The Sea

One person who has no other, either son or brother, yet there is no end to all his toil, and his eyes are never satisfied with riches, so that he never asks, "For whom am I toiling and depriving myself of pleasure?" This also is vanity and an unhappy business. Two are better than one, because they have a good reward for their toil. For if they fall, one will lift up his fellow. But woe to him who is alone when he falls and has not another to lift him up! Again, if two lie together, they keep warm, but how can one keep warm alone? And though a man might prevail against one who is alone, two will withstand him—a threefold cord is not quickly broken.

Ecclesiastes 4:8-12

Again I say to you, if two of you agree on earth about anything they ask, it will be done for them by my Father in heaven. For where two or three are gathered in my name, there am I in the midst of them.

Matthew 18:19-20

day 14

For just as the body is one and has many members, and all the members of the body, though many, are one body, so it is with Christ. For by one Spirit we were all baptized into one body—Jews or Greeks, slaves or free—and all were made to drink of one Spirit.

For the body does not consist of one member but of many. If the foot should say, "Because I am not a hand, I do not belong to the body," that would not make it any less a part of the body. And if the ear should say, "Because I am not an eye, I do not belong to the body," that would not make it any less a part of the body. If the whole body were an eye, where would be the hearing? If the whole body were an ear, where would be the sense of smell? But as it is, God arranged the organs in the body, each one of them, as he chose. If all were a single organ, where would the body be? As it is, there are many parts, yet one body. The eye cannot say to the hand, "I have no need of you," nor again the head to the feet, "I have no need of you." On the contrary, the parts of the body which seem to be weaker are indispensable, and those parts of the body which we think less honorable we invest with the greater honor, and our unpresentable parts are treated with greater modesty, which our more presentable parts do not require. But God has so composed the body, giving the greater honor to the inferior part, that there may be no discord in the body, but that the members may have the same care for one another. If one member suffers, all suffer together; if one member is honored, all rejoice together.

Now you are the body of Christ and individually members of it.

I Corinthians 12:12-27

Trusting and depending on others is often difficult, especially in an individualistic culture. Is there an area in your life where you could use a helping hand? Can you take the risk and ask a friend or neighbor for help?

day 14

NO MAN IS AN ISLAND

America is a country of "rugged individualism." We cherish our individual rights and the opportunity that an individual has to get ahead. We enjoy "rags to riches" stories—a man (most often it is a man we hear about) who is self-made, risen from office boy to being head of the office and finally owning the business. We still love to watch Westerns where a good guy stands alone against the bad guys. We celebrate rugged individualism!

We forget at great peril that our country was built by individuals who had in mind "the greatest good for the greatest number." Those early leaders celebrated the worth of each person, but they also recognized that equally important was the welfare of the nation. Ben Franklin said to the signers of The Declaration of Independence, "We must all hang together, or assuredly we shall all hang separately." They knew the truth of John Donne's classic statement, "No man is an island." Nobody stands alone.

In ancient Israel the individual had a place within the community. But the individual was never set over against or ahead of the community; identity was found within the community. The greatest punishment was being ostracized from the community. The Jewish community still tries to maintain that solidarity wherever they are in the world.

Jesus established the church as a group of individuals who were bound together by the Holy Spirit and by the spirit of love. It became clear early in the life of the church that no one was going to make it alone. Everyone needed the church and it rapidly became the center of their lives. They gathered to worship and study and pray and have fellowship; then they dispersed back into the world to live their individual lives for God. They couldn't have imagined being a Christian alone.

Things have changed, at least in much of America. Too many people today think that their own individual faith is what makes the difference; the church is just another institution. Who needs it? Faith has become a very personal thing.

The number of clubs and organizations in America is endless. From service clubs to therapy groups, people are seeking community. They want to be a part of something without taking on too much responsibility. They want togetherness without losing their individuality. The theme is too often "What's in it for me?"

Jesus knew that his disciples would never make it alone. He knew that "good feelings" for one another would not be enough. He said, "This I COMMAND you, to love one another." He would have laughed (with compassion) at the question, "Who needs the church?"

Paul's great picture of the church as the body of Christ leaves out any chance of being separatist. Each part of the body needs and is dependent upon the others. We find our identity as children of God within the beloved community. We hear the words of Jesus, "For whoever would save his life will lose it; and whoever loses his life for my sake and the gospel's will save it." We do not lose ourselves in the church; we find ourselves in the church.

The church continues to celebrate the worth of the individual within the community. "No man is an island, entire of itself."

Join the beloved community!

ready to go **day 15**

Ah, who is nigh? come to me, friend or foe,
And tell me who is victor, York or Warwick?
Why ask I that? my mangled body shows,
My blood, my want of strength, my sick heart shows.
That I must yield my body to the earth
And, by my fall, the conquest to my foe.
Thus yields the cedar to the axe's edge,
Whose arms gave shelter to the princely eagle,
Under whose shade the ramping lion slept,
Whose top-branch overpeer'd Jove's spreading tree
And kept low shrubs from winter's powerful wind.
These eyes, that now are dimm'd with death's black veil,
Have been as piercing as the mid-day sun,
To search the secret treasons of the world:...
Lo, now my glory smear'd in dust and blood!
My parks, my walks, my manors that I had.
Even now forsake me, and of all my lands
Is nothing left me but my body's length.
Why, what is pomp, rule, reign, but earth and dust?
And, live we how we can, yet die we must.

Shakespeare, Henry the VI

Christ the Lord is ris'n today, Alleluia!
Sons of men and angels say, Alleluia!
Raise your joys and triumphs high, Alleluia!
Sing, ye heav'ns, and earth, reply, Alleluia!

Lives again our glorious King, Alleluia!
Where, O death, is now thy sting? Alleluia!
Once He died our souls to save, Alleluia!
Where thy victory, O grave? Alleluia!

Love's redeeming work is done, Alleluia!
Fought the fight, the battle won, Alleluia!
Death in vain forbids His rise, Alleluia!
Christ hath opened paradise, Alleluia!

Soar we now where Christ hath led, Alleluia!
Foll'wing our exalted Head, Alleluia!
Made like Him, like Him we rise, Alleluia!
Ours the cross, the grave, the skies, Alleluia.

Charles Wesley, Christ the Lord is Risen Today

But we would not have you ignorant, brethren, concerning those who are asleep, that you may not grieve as others do who have no hope. For since we believe that Jesus died and rose again, even so, through Jesus, God will bring with him those who have fallen asleep.

1 Thessalonians 4:13-14

Then two men will be in the field; one will be taken and one left. Two women will be grinding at the mill; one will be taken and one left. Therefore, stay awake, for you do not know on what day your Lord is coming. But know this, that if the master of the house had known in what part of the night the thief was coming, he would have stayed awake and would not have let his house be broken into. Therefore you also must be ready, for the Son of Man is coming at an hour you do not expect.

Matthew 24:40-44

Truly, truly, I say to you, unless a grain of wheat falls into the earth and dies, it remains alone; but if it dies, it bears much fruit. He who loves his life loses it, and he who hates his life in this world will keep it for eternal life.

John 12:24-25

day 15

day 15

READY TO GO

Two of the greatest men of this century, Pope John XXIII and Dr. Martin Luther King, Jr., according to their biographers, lived life with the knowledge that death was always just around the corner. Their conversations and speeches just prior to their deaths reflect their faith and their readiness to go.

It is a reassuring experience to have someone who is facing death say calmly and peacefully, "I'm ready to go." My mother before her surgery for cancer (which, shortly after, took her life) said to me and my brother, "I'm ready to go! I've lived too long and I'm ready to see Dad" (who had died 16 years earlier). It was a powerful testimony for two sons.

All of us would live better lives if we lived as though "ready to go." Not fearing what the future brings enables us to live with much greater freedom in the present. Being ever aware of our mortality is equally important and gives us greater regard for NOW. Carpe diem, seize the moment!

My wife and I, before going to each of the two pastorates that we have served, decided that we should, like the good Pope, go with our bags packed, ready to go. Each move was a difficult decision and we had no idea how things would work out; we expected a lot of pressure. Our decision brought a much greater freedom to do and say what was needed. If necessary, we were "ready to go."

It is not just in facing death that we need to be ready to go; it is throughout our lives. The ability to pull up stakes, to move, to start over again, believing that God will go with us, is an unbelievable freedom.

"Keeping our bags packed" is only a problem when we have too many bags. Experience in travelling teaches us that we would be much better off without so much luggage, but most of us carry extra stuff, just in case. Never can tell when we might need that new little gizmo, so we burden ourselves with too many bags. In Latin the word for luggage is impedimenta. That's what luggage is for most of us, an impediment.

Our consumer economy tends to weigh us all down with far too many things; we are tied to material possessions. When it comes time to move, we cannot believe how much stuff we have accumulated. It is then that we wish we could, like the proverbial Arab, "fold our tents and quietly steal away," but our tents are too loaded.

We have been sold a bill of goods, quite literally.

The Boy Scout movement is known for its motto, "Be prepared." The Scouts try to teach young people to plan and think ahead so that they will be better prepared to meet whatever emergency arises. To be prepared is to be ready to go.

Paul wanted the church in Thessalonica to know what lay ahead so they would be prepared and ready to go. "But we would not have you ignorant, brethren, concerning those who are asleep, that you may not grieve as others do who have no hope."

It was that same faith that prepared Pope John XXIII and Dr. King to meet death with equanimity. It is that same faith that prepares you and me to face life and death with equanimity; it is that same faith that prepares us and enables us to be "ready to go."

what is love? day 16

Love can't be pinned down by a definition, and it certainly can't be proved, any more than anything else important in life can be proved. Love is people, is a person. A friend of ours, Hugh Bishop of Mirfield, says in one of his books: "Love is not an emotion. It is a policy." Those words have often helped me when all my feelings were unlovely. In a summer household as large as ours I often have to act on those words. I am slowly coming to understand with my heart as well as my head that love is not a feeling. It is a person."

Madeleine L'Engle, A Circle Of Quiet

Love is not a feeling. Many, many people possessing a feeling of love and even acting in response to that feeling act in all manner of unloving and destructive ways. On the other hand, a genuinely loving individual will often take loving and constructive action toward a person he or she consciously dislikes, actually feeling no love toward the person at the time and perhaps even finding the person repugnant in some way.

Scott Peck, The Road Less Traveled

The idea expressed in the Biblical "Love thy neighbor as thyself!" implies that respect for one's own integrity and uniqueness, love for and understanding of one's own self, can not be separated from respect for and love and understanding of another individual. The love for my own self is inseparably connected with the love for any other self.

We have come now to the basic psychological premises on which the conclusions of our argument are built. Generally, these premises are as follows: not only others, but we ourselves are the "object" of our feelings and attitudes; the attitudes toward others and toward ourselves, far from being contradictory, are basically conjunctive. With regard to the problem under discussion this means: Love of others and love of ourselves are not alternatives. On the contrary, an attitude of love toward themselves will be found in all those who are capable of loving others. Love, in principle, is indivisible as far as the connection between "objects" and one's own self is concerned. Genuine love is an expression of productiveness and implies care, respect, responsibility, and knowledge. It is not an "affect" in the sense of being affected by somebody, but an active striving for the growth and happiness of the loved person, rooted in one's own capacity to love.

To love is an expression of one's power to love, and to love somebody is the actualization and concentration of this power with regard to one person.

Erich Fromm, Man For Himself

Let me not to the marriage of true minds
Admit impediments. Love is not love
Which alters when it alteration finds,
Or bends with the remover to remove:
O no! it is an ever-fixed mark
That looks on tempests and is never shaken;
It is the star to every wandering bark,
Whose worth's unknown,
although his height be taken.
Love's not Time's fool,
though rosy lips and cheeks
Within his bending sickle's compass come:
Love alters not with his brief hours and weeks,
But bears it out even to the edge of doom.
If this be error and upon me proved,
I never writ, nor no man ever loved.

William Shakespeare, Sonnet 116

If I speak in the tongues of men and of angels, but have not love, I am a noisy gong or a clanging cymbal. And if I have prophetic powers, and understand all mysteries and all knowledge, and if I have all faith, so as to remove mountains, but have not love, I am nothing. f I give away all I have, and if I deliver my body to be burned, but have not love, I

day 16

gain nothing. Love is patient and kind; love is not jealous or boastful; it is not arrogant or rude. Love does not insist on its own way; it is not irritable or resentful; it does not rejoice at wrong, but rejoices in the right. Love bears all things, believes all things, hopes all things, endures all things. Love never ends; as for prophecies, they will pass away; as for tongues, they will cease; as for knowledge, it will pass away.

I Corinthians 13:4-8

This is my commandment, that you love one another as I have loved you. Greater love has no man than this, that a man lay down his life for his friends. You are my friends if you do what I command you. No longer do I call you servants, for the servant does not know what his master is doing; but I have called you friends, for all that I have heard from my Father I have made known to you. You did not choose me, but I chose you and appointed you that you should go and bear fruit and that your fruit should abide; so that whatever you ask the Father in my name, he may give it to you. This I command you, to love one another.

John 15:12-17

day 16

WHAT IS LOVE?

A psychiatrist once asked me, "Do you like everybody?" My immediate answer was, "Heavens, no!" His reply was, "Then why do you think everybody should like you?" Good question!

It was the beginning for me of facing the fact that liking and loving are quite different. Liking is having a natural affinity for someone or something. Liking has to do with tastes, predispositions, and prejudices.

Love is quite different, at least in the New Testament sense. The Greek word *agape* is defined as invincible good will, unconquerable benevolence. Agape is God's love for us. "In this is love, not that we first loved God but that God first loved us."

Madaleine L'Engle quotes a friend saying, "Love is a policy." Love is different than liking. We are supposed to love someone that we may not like because love is a policy. As God loves us in spite of ourselves, we try to love others in the same way. We try to be benevolent even when we don't feel like it, even when our natural prejudices or predispositions say, "I don't like him."

Unfortunately our culture is hooked on romantic love and blurs the distinction between loving and liking. Romantic love is something that happens to you; you fall in love. Romantic love is a feeling. "Birds sing, bells ring," we are overwhelmed. No wonder we make irrational decisions about our love relationships.

If love is a policy, then you try to love someone even when you don't feel up to it at the moment, even when you don't like him/her. If love is a policy, then it is more an act of the will than an emotional response. You can will to love someone even when you don't want to love them or don't feel like it.

St. Paul uses the word *agape* when he writes his famous passage: "Love bears all things, believes all things, hopes all things, endures all things. Love never ends." A love like that takes every bit of benevolence and good will we can muster. It certainly is not dependent upon the emotional response of the moment or how you happen to be feeling.

I suspect that Jesus commanded us to love one another because he knew how fragile and weak we are and that, left to ourselves, we would quit loving as soon as we quit liking. It is not just a suggestion he makes; it is not a recommendation. It is a command! "Love one another even as I have loved you."

L'Engle suggests in addition that "love is a person." Yes, indeed, and it is the particularity of that person that we love. Five-foot-two, eyes of blue, dimpled cheeks, wonderful smile, good sense of humor, etc., etc. We don't love in general; love is focused on a person and that person's particularities.

It is unfortunate that those same particularities are the troublemakers, for we all have our warts and blemishes. Love, however, takes the good with the bad, "for better or for worse, for richer or for poorer, in sickness and in health."

Love is most especially wonderful because it is a gift. There is nothing we can do to earn it. We can only respond and give the gift of our own love in return. Because we have been loved, we are able to love. What a wondrous thing is love!

"Beloved, let us love one another; for love is of God."

searchers day 17

This is a book born in my heart, born in the pain of ending one life and beginning another, born in the excitement of the continuing search for life's meaning. Some people do not have to search, they find their niche early in life and rest there, seemingly contented and resigned. They do not seem to ask much of life, sometimes they do not seem to take it seriously. At times I envy them, but usually I do not understand them. Seldom do they understand me.

I am one of the searchers. There are, I believe, millions of us. We are not unhappy, but neither are we really content. We continue to explore life, hoping to uncover its ultimate secret. We continue to explore ourselves, hoping to understand. We like to walk along the beach, we are drawn by the ocean, taken by its power, its unceasing motion, its mystery and unspeakable beauty. We like forests and mountains, deserts and hidden rivers, and the lonely cities as well. Our sadness is as much a part of our lives as is our laughter. To share our sadness with one we love is perhaps as great a joy as we can know—unless it be to share our laughter.

We searchers are ambitious only for life itself, for everything beautiful it can provide. Most of all we want to love and be loved. We want to live in a relationship that will not impede our wandering, nor prevent our search, nor lock us in prison walls; that will take us for what little we have to give. We do not want to prove ourselves to another or to compete for love.

This is a book for wanderers, dreamers and lovers, for lonely men and women who dare to ask of life everything good and beautiful. It is for those who are too gentle to live among wolves.

James Kavanaugh,
There Are Men Too Gentle To Live Among Wolves

There are more things in heaven and earth, Horatio, than are dreamt of in your philosophy.

Shakespeare, Hamlet

O Lord, our Lord,
how majestic is thy name in all the earth!
Thou whose glory above the heavens is chanted
by the mouth of babes and infants,
thou hast founded a bulwark
because of thy foes,
to still the enemy and the avenger.
When I look at thy heavens, the
work of thy fingers,
the moon and the stars which
thou hast established:
what is man that thou are mindful of him,
and the son of man that thou dost care for him?
Yet thou hast made him little less than God,
and dost crown him with glory and honor.
Thou hast given him dominion over
the works of thy hands;

thou hast put all things under his feet,
all sheep and oxen,

and also the beasts of the field,

the birds of the air, and the fish of the sea,
whatever passes along the paths of the sea.
O Lord, our Lord,
how majestic is thy name in all
the earth!

Psalm 8

Seek the Lord while he may be found.
Call upon him while he is near.
Let the wicked forsake his ways
And the unrighteous his thoughts.
Let him return to the Lord, that he
may have mercy on him,
And to our God, for he will
abundantly pardon.

Isaiah 55:6-7

day 17

So I became great and surpassed all who were before me in Jerusalem; also my wisdom remained with me. And whatever my eyes desired I did not keep from them; I kept my heart from no pleasure, for my heart found pleasure in all my toil, and this was my reward for all my toil. Then I considered all that my hands had done and the toil I had spent in doing it, and behold, all was vanity and a striving after wind, and there was nothing to be gained under the sun.

Ecclesiastes 2:9-11

And it shall come to pass afterward,
that I will pour out my spirit on all flesh;
Your old men shall dream dreams,
and your young men shall see visions.

Joel 2:28

Ask, and it will be given you; seek, and you will find; knock, and it will be opened to you. For every one who asks receives, and he who seeks finds, and to him who knocks it will be opened.

Matthew 7:7-8

Now we see in a mirror dimly, but then face to face. Now I know in part; then I shall understand fully, even as I have been fully understood.

I Corinthians 13:12

day 17

SEARCHERS

Something within me resonates with James Kavanaugh. I feel myself in tune with him without knowing exactly why. Perhaps it is because as I get older I feel more open about the mystery of life. Perhaps it is because I see myself as a "wanderer, dreamer, and lover." Perhaps it is because I love the mountains and the sea. Perhaps it is because as an older man I know much better what it means to share sadness as well as laughter with someone I love. Resonate is accurate.

Our pluralistic culture encourages us to water everything down to the lowest common denominator, so we end up relativizing important truths. I cherish, therefore, the statement in the Presbyterian Book of Order which reads, "no opinion is more pernicious or more absurd than that which brings truth and falsehood upon a level, and represents it as of no consequence what a man's opinions are. On the contrary, we are persuaded that there is an inseparable connection between faith and practice, truth and duty. Otherwise, it would be of no consequence either to discover truth or to embrace it" (Form of Government, Chapter 3, Par. 4).

In spite of the above or maybe because of it, it is fun to sit around and discuss "the meaning of life" with those of much different persuasions and alternative lifestyles. If there is an openness and a desire to share, then we can truly be searchers together, and the dialogue is instructive.

There is a bit of Odysseus in each of us—born to wander, born to search for the right place, the deepest truth, the best relationships. We never grow too old to dream of what might have been and of what is yet to be and of what we still might become. Everyone wants to be a lover—the thought is daring—of some special person in some special place and in some special way. "Wanderers, dreamers and lovers"—why not?

It is possible that, like the writer of Ecclesiastes, we will end up saying, "all was vanity and a striving after wind, and there was nothing to be gained under the sun." But it is most likely that we will end up agreeing with Paul, "Now I see in a mirror dimly, but then face to face. Now I know in part; then I shall understand even as I have been fully understood."

Our faith, or lack of it, colors our point of view. Was the search worth it or not? More people than I care to think of have ended up cynical and despairing. Others, believing that God is with them throughout their lives, go to their graves still searching, but rejoicing in the gift of openness to what life brings.

Life is enriched by open-minded searching. Christians believe that Jesus is "the way, the truth, and the life." Since there are no clear definitions written in stone of what that text means, we keep on searching. And we laugh and cry, together, rejoicing that God has not left us "cosmic orphans." Thanks be to God!

the best things in the worst times **day 18**

For everything there is a season, and a time for every matter under heaven:

> a time to be born, and a time to die;
> a time to plant, and a time to pluck up what is planted;
> a time to kill, and a time to heal;
> a time to break down, and a time to build up;
> a time to weep, and a time to laugh;
> a time to mourn, and a time to dance;
> a time to cast away stones, and a time to gather stones together;
> a time to embrace, and a time to refrain from embracing;
> a time to seek, and a time to lose;
> a time to keep, and a time to cast away;
> a time to rend, and a time to sew;
> a time to keep silence, and a time to speak;
> a time to love, and a time to hate;
> a time for war, and a time for peace.

Ecclesiastes 3:1-8

And there he came to a cave, and lodged there; and behold, the word of the Lord came to him, and he said to him, "What are you doing here, Elijah?" He said, "I have been very jealous for the Lord, the God of hosts; for the people of Israel have forsaken thy covenant, thrown down thy altars, and slain thy prophets with the sword; and I, even I only, am left; and they seek my life to take it away."

And he said, "Go forth, and stand upon the mount before the Lord." And, behold, the Lord passed by, and a great and strong wind rent the mountains, and broke in pieces the rocks before the Lord, but the Lord was not in the wind; and after the wind, an earthquake, but the Lord was not in the earthquake; and after the earthquake a fire, but the Lord was not in the fire; and after the fire a still small voice.

And when Elijah heard it, he wrapped his face in his mantle and went out and stood at the entrance of the cave. And behold, there came a voice to him, and said, "What are you doing here, Elijah?" He said, "I have been very jealous for the Lord, the God of hosts; for the people of Israel have forsaken thy covenant, thrown down thy altars, and slain thy prophets with the sword; and I, even I only, am left; and they seek my life to take it away."

And the Lord said to him, "Go, return on your way to Damascus; and when you arrive, you shall anoint Hazael to be king over Syria; and Jehu the son of Nimshi you shall anoint to be king over Israel; and Elisha the son of Shapat of Abelmeholah you shall anoint to be prophet in your place. And him who escapes from the sword of Hazael shall Jehu slay; and him who escapes from the sword of Jehu shall Elisha slay. Yet I will leave seven thousand in Israel, all the knees that have not bowed to Baal, and every mouth that has not kissed him."

I Kings 19:9-18

And let us not grow weary in well-doing, for in due season we shall reap, if we do not lose heart. So then, as we have opportunity, let us do good to all men, and especially to those who are of the household of God.

Galatians 5:9-10

But we have this treasure in earthen vessels, to show that the transcendent power belongs to God and not to us. We are afflicted in every way, but not crushed; perplexed, but not driven to despair; persecuted, but not forsaken; struck down, but not destroyed; always carrying in the body the death of Jesus, so that the life of Jesus may also be manifest in our bodies. For while we live we are always being given up to death for Jesus' sake, so that the life of Jesus may be manifested in our mortal flesh. So death is at work in us, but life in you.

II Corinthians 4:7-12

day 18

Think of some of the worst times you've experienced during your life. How were you able to persevere through those difficult times? Does your faith help you to be your best during such times?

day 18

THE BEST THINGS IN THE WORST TIMES

In the Chapel of Staunton Harold in the English Midlands there is a plaque which reads: "In the year 1653, when all things sacred were throughout ye nation either demolished or profaned, Sir Robert Shirley, Baronet, founded this church: whose singular praise it is to have done the best things in the worst times, and hoped them in the most calamitous."

There is little else we know about Robert Shirley, but what else do we need to know? What a marvelous tribute—"to have done the best things in the worst times." Every age has its detractors who say these are the worst times. Voices all around us today are saying, "Things couldn't be much worse. What's the use?"

Compassion fatigue is comparatively new language today among social scientists but the reality has been around a long time. It is hard to stay compassionate and not to become cynical. It is hard not to tire out and give up in the face of overwhelming odds. It is difficult to continue doing "the best things in the worst times."

Was Robert Shirley motivated by faith? Perhaps, but we don't know. Perhaps some of us are blessed with that kind of faith and endurance from birth, but most of us struggle. We have to work at maturing in faith and learning to persevere when things don't go our way. We marvel at those who continue to "do the best things in the worst times."

We know only too well the words of Paul, "We have this treasure in earthen vessels." What we would like more of is his faith: "We are afflicted in every way, but not crushed; perplexed, but not driven to despair; persecuted, but not forsaken; struck down, but not destroyed."

That faith is available to us today just as much as it was to men and women of old. Most of us will have to continue to work at it. We will have to worship and study and pray and seek the fellowship of other Christians lest we lose it by going alone. In the struggle with others of similar concern we are most apt to keep our perspective about doing "the best things in the worst times."

Compassion fatigue is especially brought on by melancholy. We lose our sense of hope when we think that we are going it alone. No less a figure than Elijah gave up and withdrew, crying out to the Lord, "... I, even I only, am left; and they seek my life to take it away." But God would not accept that. "Go, return... I will leave at least 7000 in Israel."

Like Elijah we sometimes feel alone and want to run away, but we can't. The problems of the world and the responsibility of doing "the best things in the worst times" are ours. They won't go away, but neither does God.

So, then, "let us not grow weary in well-doing, for in due season we shall reap, if we do not lose heart."

finding meaning under any circumstances **day 19**

We who lived in concentration camps can remember the men who walked through the huts comforting others, giving away their last piece of bread. They may have been few in number, but they offer sufficient proof that everything can be taken from a man but one thing: the last of the human freedoms—to choose one's attitude in any given set of circumstances, to choose one's way.

And there were always choices to make. Every day, every hour, offered the opportunity to make a decision, a decision which determined whether you would or would not submit to those powers which threatened to rob you of your very self, your inner freedom; which determined whether or not you would become the plaything of circumstance, renouncing freedom and dignity to become molded into the form of the typical inmate...

Even though conditions such as lack of sleep, insufficient food and various mental stresses may suggest that the inmates were bound to react in certain ways, in the final analysis it becomes clear that the sort of person the prisoner became was the result of an inner decision, and not the result of camp influences alone. Fundamentally, therefore, any man can, even under such circumstances, decide what shall become of him—mentally and spiritually. He may retain his human dignity even in a concentration camp. Dostoevski said once, "There is only one thing that I dread; not to be worthy of my sufferings." These words came frequently to my mind after I became acquainted with those martyrs whose behavior in camp, whose suffering and death, bore witness to the fact that the last inner freedom cannot be lost. It can be said that they were worthy of their sufferings; the way they bore their suffering was a genuine inner achievement. It is this spiritual freedom—which cannot be taken away—that makes life meaningful and purposeful.

Viktor E. Frankl, Man's Search For Meaning

While visiting at the home of Mr. and Mrs.——— today little Ralph felt it incumbent upon himself to entertain me by putting the family dog through his tricks. I have already forgotten the breed of the dog, but his shaggy locks covered his eyes so completely that he seemed to be without eyesight. Ralph told me with great eagerness that the dog would go blind if his locks were cut to improve his eyesight. Thus nature adjusts herself to her own inadequacies, and women of the future may run the peril of deafness if they uncover their ears.

Ralph's dog gave me the clue to much of our irreligion. The eyes of so many people have been covered by superstitions and illusions that they are not strong enough to preserve their sight in the daylight of knowledge. Freed from their superstitions, they are blinded in the very moment that they are given an unhindered view. They could see beauty while they lived in twilight, but a brilliant light obscures life's beauty and meaning.

Of course the eye may ultimately adjust itself to the brilliance of the light, and as men grow accustomed to the concrete and specific objects which distract them on first sight, they will learn again to view the whole scene and to regard all things in their relationships.

It is in relationships and in totalities that life's meaning is revealed.

Reinhold Niebuhr, Leaves From The Notebook Of A Tamed Cynic

Surely he has borne our griefs
and carried our sorrows;
yet we esteemed him stricken,
smitten by God, and afflicted.
But he was wounded for our transgressions,
he was bruised for our iniquities;
upon him was the chastisement that made us
whole and with his stripes we are healed.
All we like sheep have gone astray; we
have turned every one to his own way;
and the Lord has laid on him

day 19

the iniquity of us all.
He was oppressed, and he was afflicted;
yet he opened not his mouth;
like a lamb that is led to the slaughter,
and like a sheep before its shearers is
dumb, so he opened not his mouth.

Isaiah 53:4-7

Rejoice always, pray without ceasing, give thanks in all circumstances; for this is the will of God in Christ Jesus for you.

1 Thessalonians 5:16-18

Every one then who hears these words of mine and does them will be like a wise man who built his house upon the rock; and the rain fell, and the floods came, and the winds blew and beat upon that house, but it did not fall, because it had been founded on the rock. And every one who hears these words of mine and does not do them will be like a foolish man who built his house upon the sand; and the rain fell, and the floods came, and the winds blew and beat against that house, and it fell; and great was the fall of it.

Matthew 7:24-27

Now Jesus stood before the governor; and the governor asked him, "Are you the King of the Jews?" Jesus said to him, "You have said so." But when he was accused by the chief priests and elders, he made no answer. Then Pilate said to him, "Do you not hear how many things they testify against you?" But he gave him no answer, not even to a single charge; so that the governor wondered greatly.

Matthew 27:11-14

day 19

FINDING MEANING UNDER ANY CIRCUMSTANCES

My first job in the ministry was as a Chaplain at Presbyterian Hospital in Philadelphia. Part of my assignment was to call at a convalescent home in the suburbs. It was not a task that I looked forward to until I had done it once. Thereafter I looked forward to my day "in the country" because I met Miss Berger.

The nurses told me about Miss Berger before I had my first visit with her. She was paralyzed from the waist down. She had been in the same room in the same bed for 53 years. That blew my mind; I was only 25 years old. What would she be like? What could she be like? She was amazing!

Those who went in to see and to minister to Miss Berger found themselves being ministered to by her. I had never seen a livelier, happier, sweeter spirit. The same bed, the same room—53 years. About the most she could do for herself was brush her teeth, comb her hair—personal hygiene.

But what she did for others was incredible. Miss Berger had chosen under the most trying circumstances to be cheerful. It was as though she was living testimony to the words of Jesus, "In the world you have tribulation, but be of good cheer, I have overcome the world." She was of good cheer and she had overcome her terrible disability with an attitude that brought healing and good cheer to whomever visited her. All these years later I still remember her wonderful spirit and attitude.

She was clear proof of Viktor Frankl's statement about certain prisoners: "they offer sufficient proof that everything can be taken from a man but one thing: the last of the human freedoms—to choose one's attitude in any given set of circumstances, to choose one's way."

Most of us are fortunate that we do not have to make such choices. We are not disabled, imprisoned, or chronically ill. To the contrary we are among the most blessed people on earth, at least in part because we live in America. But Americans are noted for complaining about life. Griping and "bitching" are as American as apple pie. We joke that someone is recovering from illness when he or she begins to complain a bit.

We can justify some complaining as a healthy release from the tensions of life, but what counts most is our attitude when we are no longer able to control the circumstances in which we find ourselves. The last of our freedoms is the most wonderful of all—the ability to choose our attitude, to retain our dignity.

Convalescent homes may offer the best example of how we choose our attitude. Very few of us in our earlier years anticipate or desire ever ending up in an "old folk's home." If the day ever comes that for one reason or another we arrive in such a place, decision time has come.

What will we be like—cheerful, grouchy, complaining, helpful, friendly, withdrawn? The list of adjectives is endless; it reads like the Boy Scout Law. Unfortunately, time seems to be endless, so what will we choose? What will our attitude be? The choice is never easy, but IT IS OUR CHOICE.

"In the world you have tribulation, but be of good cheer, I have overcome the world."

therapy of breadbaking day 20

If so, let me try to sweeten the cup. For there are compensations, not immediately apparent. Bring together four or five committed bread bakers, loosen them up with a strong pot of tea, and listen closely as they talk about the subtle, far-reaching, and distinctively positive changes that can take place when you begin to bake regularly...

First, on the personal level, there's the purely therapeutic effect. Watch a four-year-old burst in the door after a long morning with his buddies, still exultant, talking nonstop, but exhausted, too, from the sustained stress of it all. Watch him fall with instinctive good sense on a pile of play-dough, and pull, push, pummel and squeeze until finally all the tension has flowed out through his fingertips and he is at peace. Watch him, and wonder why on earth grown-ups shouldn't have access to the same very healing, very basic kind of activity. And, in fact, they can. For kneading bread dough, forming it into coffee-cake wreaths or cottage loaves or long baguettes affords exactly this kind of satisfaction.

Good breadbaking is much more, though, than just a good outlet. At certain critical junctures, you really have got to block out extraneous goings-on and attend meticulously to small details. Far from being onerous, these more exacting phases of the baking process can also be the most calming—precisely because they do require such powerful concentration. And the very fact that so much of oneself is called upon, in the way of artistry and resourcefulness, makes the whole business that much more gratifying—enhances the quality of life over-all.

Laurel Robertson with Carol Flinders and Bronwen Godfrey, The Laurel's Kitchen Bread Book

Finally, brethren, whatever is true, whatever is honorable, whatever is just, whatever is pure, whatever is lovely, whatever is gracious, if there is any excellence, if there is anything worthy of praise, think about these things.

Philippians 4:8

And the tempter came and said to him, "If you are the Son of God, command these stones to become loaves of bread." But he answered, "It is written, 'Man shall not live by bread alone, but by every word that proceeds from the mouth of God.'"

Matthew 4:3,4

Give us this day our daily bread.

Matthew 6:11

So they said to him, "Then what sign do you do, that we may see, and believe you? What work do you perform? Our fathers ate manna in the wilderness; as it is written, 'He gave them bread from heaven to eat.'" Jesus said to them, "Truly, truly, I say to you, it was not Moses who gave you the bread from heaven; my Father gives you the true bread from heaven. For the bread of God is that which comes down from heaven, and gives life to the world." They said to him, "Lord, give us this bread always."

Jesus said to them, "I am the bread of life; he who comes to me shall not hunger, and he who believes in me shall never thirst. ...Your fathers ate the manna in the wilderness, and they died. This is the bread which comes down from heaven, that a man may eat of it and not die. I am the living bread which came down from heaven; if any one eats of this bread, he will live forever; and the bread which I shall give for the life of the world is my flesh."

John 6:30-35, 48-51

day 20

Now as they were eating, Jesus took bread, and blessed, and broke it, and gave it to his disciples and said, "Take, eat, this is my body." And he took a cup, and when he had given thanks he gave it to them, saying, "Drink of it, all of you; for this is my blood of the covenant, which is poured out for many for the forgiveness of sins. I tell you I shall not drink again of this fruit of the vine until the day when I drink it new with you in my Father's kingdom."

Matthew 26:26-29

Your boasting is not good. Do you not know that a little leaven leavens the whole lump? Cleanse out the old leaven that you may be a new lump, as you really are unleavened. For Christ, our paschal lamb, has been sacrificed. Let us, therefore, celebrate the festival, not with the old leaven, the leaven of malice and evil, but with the unleavened bread of sincerity and truth.

I Corinthians 5:6-8

day 20

THE THERAPY OF BREADBAKING

Learning to bake bread was for me an exhilarating experience; I had never done anything like it. My teacher was a person who exuded confidence about the whole process and loved to eat the finished product (he didn't like cleaning up, however). He left no doubt that I could do it. So I started.

Carefully measuring out the ingredients and carefully watching the yeast rise and carefully watching the temperature was all part of a necessary attention to detail; meticulous best describes the process. But the magical part was the kneading. My teacher had done it with vigor and verve, so I did my best to emulate him.

Pushing and pulling and pounding and poking, I really got into it. Driven by thoughts of people who had made me mad and stressful details of parish life, I let that dough have it. If the secret was in the kneading, I could handle that. That dough never knew what hit it. When I was done, I could almost giggle. All sorts of frustrations had exited through my hands. I loved it. From that moment on I was a convert, long before I ate my first home-made loaf.

Very seldom in the life of a minister do you get a sense of completion or control. You're never quite certain what is going to happen with counselees, with young people, with young marrieds. Trying to shape a parish into something pleasing to God is fraught with a sense of guilt because you're not doing enough or you're not doing it right. Seldom do you see a finished product.

No wonder shaping a loaf of bread gives such a sense of satisfaction. Roll it, pat it, poke it—not quite right; roll it, pat it, poke it again. There it is—before your very eyes; you can control it—the size, shape, color, texture, taste. You have created something, entire and complete. It doesn't argue, it doesn't fight back, it doesn't think it is smarter than you are, it doesn't even think it is better than you are. It is as famous chef Yvonne Tarr says, "...an honest loaf, an object with a presence, a fragrance, a substance, a taste, some would even say a soul..."

Our lives are like those loaves in some ways. The internal and external pressures of our lives mold and shape us, too; we are kneaded, patted, pushed, and pulled into a variety of shapes. We wish we weren't so pliable. I doubt that St. Paul baked bread, but he obviously understood the process when he wrote, "Don't let the world around you squeeze you into its own mold, but let God remold your mind from within." Look out or you may be a loaf.

After many years I still have that exhilarating experience as I bake bread—push, pull, poke, pound. "Take that, Mrs. Smith. So much for you, Mr. Jones." The fun and the joy that goes with the kneading once again brings me that marvelous sense of release.

More importantly, I am reminded that my own life is shaped by outside forces all too easily and I am forced to ask again, "What am I doing to let God remold my mind from within?"

As Laurel Robertson wrote, "The very fact that so much of oneself is called upon, in the way of artistry and resourcefulness, makes the whole business that much more gratifying—enhances the quality of life over-all."

Every preacher should try the therapy of bread-baking. And whoever you are, you'll enjoy it.

you can't go home again day 21

Faith involves leaving home. Obeying a fresh call of God means leaving home. Leaving our provisional homes, roles, relationships, lands, belief systems, life styles—all, to go out in search of an abiding homeland. Don't misunderstand me. Abraham and Sarah left home together. For most people leaving home in response to a fresh call from God does not mean getting separated and divorced, leaving one's job and house, although it did mean those things for me. Leaving home as a faithful response is for everybody. The particularities of our calling and our leaving vary as richly and diversely as do our lives. Leaving home means leaving imperatives and agendas that are no longer healthy, fulfilling, fitting. Leaving home means moving out into a transitional period, which is characterized by renting rather than owning, one way rather than round trip, anywhere rather than a known somewhere. It is frightening, scary, risky, promising and energizing...

It is painful to leave home. Leaving is grieving, for our losses are real and there is tragedy in our lives as well as transformation. There is death as well as rebirth. Indeed, unless there is death there can be no rebirth. Rebirth comes only out of what is dying. We mustn't dote on the past, because doting distorts the present, but grieving allows the past to be gathered, celebrated, offered, and released. Grieving allows the future to be born in us and those new yearnings to live and shape our tomorrows.

Robert A. Raines, Going Home

But Caleb quieted the people before Moses, and said, "Let us go up at once, and occupy it; for we are well able to overcome it." Then the men who had gone with him said, "We are not able to go up against the people; for they are stronger than we." So they brought to the people of Israel an evil report of the land which they had spied out, saying, "The land, through which we have gone, to spy it out, is a land that devours its inhabitants; and all the people that we saw in it are men of great stature. And there we saw the Nephilim (the sons of Anak, who come from the Nephilim); and we seemed to ourselves like grasshoppers, and so we seemed to them."

Then all the congregation raised a loud cry; and the people wept that night. And all the people of Israel murmured against Moses and Aaron; the whole congregation said to them, "Would that we had died in the land of Egypt! Or would that we had died in the wilderness! Why does the Lord bring us into this land, to fall by the sword? Our wives and our little ones will become a prey; would it not be better for us to go back to Egypt?

And they said to one another, "Let us choose a captain, and go back to Egypt."

Numbers 13:30-14:4

"Hear, O Israel: The Lord our God is one Lord; and you shall love the Lord your God with all your heart, and with all your soul, and with all your might. And these words which I command you this day shall be upon your heart; and you shall teach them diligently to your children, and shall talk of them when you sit in your house, and when you walk by the way, and when you lie down, and when you rise. And you shall bind them as a sign upon your hand, and they shall be as frontlets between your eyes. And you shall write them on the doorposts of your house and on your gates.

Deuteronomy 6:4-9

day 21

As they were going along the road, a man said to him, "I will follow you wherever you go." And Jesus said to him, "Foxes have holes, and birds of the air have nests; but the Son of man has nowhere to lay his head." To another he said, "Follow me." But he said, "Lord, let me first go and bury my father." But he said to him, "Leave the dead to bury their own dead; but as for you, go and proclaim the kingdom of God." Another said, "I will follow you, Lord; but let me first say farewell to those at my home." Jesus said to him, "No one who puts his hand to the plow and looks back is fit for the kingdom of God."

Luke 9:57-62

Peter then came out with the other disciple, and they went toward the tomb. They both ran, but the other disciple outran Peter and reached the tomb first; and stooping to look in, he saw the linen cloths lying there, but he did not go in. Then Simon Peter came, following him, and went into the tomb; he saw the linen cloths lying, and the napkin, which had been on his head, not lying with the linen cloths but rolled up in a place by itself. Then the other disciple, who reached the tomb first, also went in, and he saw and believed; for as yet they did not know the scripture, that he must rise from the dead. Then the disciples went back to their homes.

John 20:3-10

day 21

YOU CAN'T GO HOME AGAIN

The year I graduated from college my father, who was disabled, asked me to drive him back to his ancestral home in Mississippi. It was one of my last chances to be with him before going to seminary and getting married, so I was pleased to do it. Though it was hard on him physically, we had an enjoyable trip as we drove from Texas all the way to Columbus, Mississippi.

When we arrived in his hometown, however, it was very depressing for him. He had been gone for almost fifteen years and the little town had changed substantially. World War II had brought a great deal of new growth. There were lots of new people and fewer of his old friends. Familiar buildings had been knocked down and new ones built. Old roads had been closed and new ones replaced them. His old home and property had changed dramatically. It was not what he hoped to see; it was bad news and it was painful for him.

At that stage of my life I was too young to realize that my father was experiencing in a very profound way the truth of which Thomas Wolfe wrote—"you can't go home again." Dad suddenly felt worse physically and he was struggling emotionally. At his insistence we cut our visit short and headed back to Texas.

Home, for most of us, is a place of meaning and significance. It represents the sights and the sounds and the smells of yesteryear. It stands for feelings of familiarity and warmth, the sense of belonging and security. Home has to do with our continuities. Home is where we head for the holidays.

"'Mid pleasures and palaces though we may roam, Be it ever so humble, there's no place like home!" (John Payne, 1823).

What we don't want to face is that, once we have left, we can never go home again. Oh yes, we can take a trip, make a pilgrimage, join the family reunion, but we can't go home again because we are different and the people and the place are, too. I saw my Dad experience that in a very depressing way.

Leaving home is part of maturing, of growing up and being on our own. It is a universal human experience and a very painful one; some people never make it. They are always looking back, wanting to return to the security of their youth, to the love of their family, to the pleasant feelings of those continuities.

When painful moments come, the human tendency is to go home again. The people of Israel wanted to return to Egypt as bad as it had been. Unbelievable? Not really! After the crucifixion, John records the fact that "the disciples went home again." They didn't know what else to do, so they tried going back. It didn't work.

The Bible reminds us that we are strangers and sojourners here on earth. We are pilgrims on a journey to "the promised land." "This earth is not our home." But we do not wish to hear the words of Jesus: "No one who puts his hand to the plow and looks back is fit for the kingdom of God."

Faith calls us to face a difficult truth—we can't go home again. We are called to move forward toward a heavenly home, a better place, one that God has prepared. Our old continuities will seem paltry beside that new reality. Such a possibility leads us to sing with joy the words of an old spiritual, "I'm going home to see my Father."

lip-smacking, exuhberant delight day 22

Is it not by his high superfluousness we know
Our God? For to equal a need
Is natural, animal, mineral: but to fling
Rainbows over the rain
And beauty above the moon,
and secret rainbows
On the domes of sea-shells,
And make the necessary embrace of breeding
Beautiful also as fire,
Not even the weeds to multiply
without blossom
Nor the birds without music:
There is the great humaneness
at the heart of things,
The extravagant kindness, the fountain
Humanity can understand, and
would flow likewise
If power and desire were perchmates.

Robinson Jeffers, The Excesses of God

Glory be to God for dappled things—
For skies of couple-colour as a brinded cow;
For rose-moles all in stipple
upon trout that swim;
Fresh-firecoal chestnut-falls, finches' wings;
Landscape plotted and pierced
fold, fallow, and plough;
And all trades, their gear and tackle and trim.
All things counter, original, spare, strange;
Whatever is fickle, freckled (who knows how?)
With swift, slow; sweet, sour; adazzle, dim;
He fathers-forth whose beauty is past change:
Praise him.

Gerald Manley Hopkins, Pied Beauty

Then God said, "Let us make man in our image, after our likeness; and let them have dominion over the fish of the sea, and over the birds of the air, and over the cattle, and over all the earth, and over every creeping thing that creeps upon the earth." So God created man in his own image, in the image of God he created him; male and female he created them. And God blessed them, and God said to them, "Be fruitful and multiply, and fill the earth and subdue it; and have dominion over the fish of the sea and over the birds of the air and over every living thing that moves upon the earth." And God said, "Behold, I have given you every plant yielding seed which is upon the face of all the earth, and every tree with seed in its fruit; you shall have them for food. And to every beast of the earth, and to every bird of the air, and to everything that creeps on the earth, everything that has the breath of life, I have given every green plant for food." And it was so. And God saw everything that he had made, and behold, it was very good.

Genesis 1:26-31

The heavens are telling the glory of God;
and the firmament proclaims his handiwork.
Day to day pours forth speech,
and night to night declares knowledge.
There is no speech, nor are there words;
their voice is not heard;
yet their voice goes out through all the earth,
and their words to the end of the world.

Psalm 19:1-4

But to what shall I compare this generation? It is like children sitting in the market places and calling to their playmates,
"We piped to you, and you did not dance; we wailed, and you did not mourn."
For John came neither eating nor drinking, and they say, "He has a demon"; the Son of man came eating and drinking, and they say, "Behold, a glutton and a drunkard, a friend of tax collectors and sinners!" Yet wisdom is justified by his deeds.

Matthew 11:16-19

day 22

Can one be deeply religious while also delighting in life's pleasures? Do you know anyone who exemplifies this rare combination? Does your spirituality cause you to take more or less delight in life?

day 22

LIP-SMACKING, EXUBERANT DELIGHT

Question 1 of *The Westminster Shorter Catechism*: "What is the chief end of man?" Answer: "Man's chief end is to glorify God and enjoy him forever." An immediate question arises from deep within us—How do we enjoy God?

Mystics and saints down through the centuries have given us an assortment of answers, too often negative. One way, often overlooked, is to enjoy life and the world God gave us. "And God saw everything that he had made, and behold, it was very good." The Hebrew is "Toth Meoth," "exceedingly, exceedingly." No wonder the characteristic Hebrew attitude toward the world was "lip-smacking delight." If God thought it was good, why shouldn't they?

The Puritans contributed a great deal to the history of our country; unfortunately they also burdened us with their guilt and their morality. A Puritan was once defined as "a person who was afraid that someone, somewhere might be having a good time." It is ironic that people of such faith could rob life of so much joy.

The American work ethic came out of Puritanism. The sovereignty of God left little room for play of any type. God was watching and keeping track, just like Santa Claus in the popular song, "He's making a list and checking it twice, gonna find out who's naughty and nice." American Christianity became more an emphasis on petty morality than a rejoicing in God's grace. Too many of us became graduates of The Institute:

Rooty-te-toot, rooty-te-toot, we're the boys from The Institute. We don't smoke, we don't chew and we don't go with girls that do. Our class won the Bible! Some people don't think we have any fun. We don't!

Hard to believe that such an attitude came out of an Old Testament that has 13 Hebrew roots found in at least 27 different words used primarily to express some aspect of joy. Terms for rejoicing in the Old Testament include "the sounds of singing, shouting, noise, uproar, and a loud voice singing praise." Physical motion was a common part of joyful expression—dancing, clapping, leaping, or stamping of feet (*The Interpreters Dictionary of the Bible*).

Where did we lose our sense of joy in the Lord? Where did faith become associated with sobriety, seriousness, and somber expressions? Where? What a tragedy that followers of a faith filled with joy seldom communicate that feeling. The church is more often associated with killjoys and spoilsports. Men stay away from the church in droves because the church is no fun.

Commitment to the cause of Christ is serious business but not without joy. We were not intended to be Junior Jesuses running around thinking that we are going to save the world. Many Christians supposedly rejoice in the fact that we are saved by faith, not by works. Living with a sense of joy and a smile on our face is more apt to win people to the cause of Christ than condemning people to Hell because they have not accepted our orthodoxy.

Life is difficult enough at best. Christians should not be adding to the burdens of others; instead they should be making lighter the burdens of others by sharing a sense of joy. Why leave all the fun to the "happy pagans?" Let us enjoy!

facing your mortality **day 23**

Fortunately, despite the fear and loneliness, I began to visit my friends, to give them the bad news and to vent my feelings. I praise the Lord for providing people who love us... As my friends and I cried together and hugged one another, I began to rebuild my hope. It was a different kind of hope from the hope of having an indefinite future on earth. Because I knew that I was loved and so would always be happy I could ask new questions. What did I want to do with each day allotted to me? I wanted to see all of my friends again. This meant going back to college. I also wanted to share special moments with friends at home. I began to plan again. Surprisingly, I soon realized that I was preparing to do many of the things that I had hoped to do when I was feeling cleansed of leukemia. Life goes on, the torch remains lit, the struggle continues.

I still feared death and the experience of dying. Is it painful? Is it lonely? But despite my fear, I accepted the fact that death would eventually take me, perhaps soon. Therefore, I had better enjoy all the days of my remaining life. And I have begun to do that now in full. I feel now as if I am in a very large city at night, perhaps around one or two in the morning. I go up and down the streets visiting night clubs where wonderful jazz is being played and friends are making merry. I am enjoying myself this evening, but I am also trying to avoid someone. That someone is Death, but he is no longer a leering skeleton in a black hood. Death is now dressed in a dapper three piece suit and carrying a walking stick. I know that he is following me and that when he finds me, I will have to leave this wonderful city and go somewhere else. But I continue, at present, to evade him, staying a few blocks out of reach. Yet, when I make a wrong turn and go down a dead end street, he will find me, put his arm around me and say, "Tough luck, Pete, it's time to go." And we'll leave without fear of each other.

Fortunately, because of the wonderful power of God's love, which is within all of us, I can enjoy the night life while hoping to see a new dawn, knowing that Paul was correct when he said: "There is nothing love cannot face; there is no limit to its faith, its hope, and its endurance. Love will never come to an end" (I Corinthians 3:7,8).

It is when we understand this that hope wells up within us and pushes us forward to the very limit of our being. When we understand and feel God's never-ending love, we can triumph over death and over all the frustrations of life on earth. It is through the experience of love that God reveals his justice to us.

Peter Findlay, The Christian Century

For within the hollow crown
That rounds the mortal temples of a king
Keeps Death his court, and there the antic sits,
Scoffing his state and grinning at his pomp,
Allowing him a breath, a little scene
To monarchize, be feared, and kill with looks,
Infusing him with self and vain conceit,
As if this flesh which walls about our life
Were brass impregnable. And humored thus,
Comes at the last, and with a little pin
Bores through his castle walls, and farewell king.
William Shakespeare, Richard II

The Lord is my shepherd, I shall not want;
he makes me lie down in green pastures.
He leads me beside still waters;
he restores my soul.
He leads me in paths of righteousness for his name's sake.
Even though I walk through the valley of the shadow of death,
I fear no evil; for thou art with me;
thy rod and thy staff, they comfort me.
Psalm 23:1-4

day 23

The years of our life are threescore and ten,
or even by reason of strength fourscore;
yet their span is but toil and trouble;
they are soon gone, and we fly away ...
So teach us to number our days
that we may get a heart of wisdom ...

Psalm 90:10, 12, 17

Jesus said to her, "I am the resurrection and the life; he who believes in me, though he die, yet shall he live, and whoever lives and believes in me shall never die. Do you believe this?"

John 11:25-26

For I am sure that neither death, nor life, nor angels, nor principalities, nor things present, nor things to come, nor powers, nor height, nor depth, nor anything else in all creation, will be able to separate us from the love of God in Christ Jesus our Lord.

Romans 8:38-39

Come now, you who say, "Today or tomorrow, we will go into such and such a town and spend a year there and trade and get gain;" whereas you do not know about tomorrow. What is your life? For you are a mist that appears for a little time and then vanishes. Instead you ought to say, "If the Lord wills, we shall live and do this or that." As it is, you boast in your arrogance. All such boasting is evil.

James 4:13-16

day 23

FACING YOUR MORTALITY

In each of the last two years I have had dramatic encounters with mortality. The first time I was told that I might have a brain tumor and the second time that I might have had a heart attack. Further testing and waiting revealed that I was o.k. No damage, no tumor, nothing to fear. What a relief!

A wonderful sense of well-being arose within me. I felt almost euphoric. My senses were alert, if not eager. Things smelled better, tasted better, looked better, felt better. Most of the things that cause anxiety and stress in the normal course of my life simply faded from view, or at least no longer seemed so important. The problems could wait. I wanted NOW. It was time "to smell the roses."

I was very lucky! Many people aren't so lucky; for them, mortality is a sudden and present reality. At root, though, mortality is a present and continuing reality in all of our lives. We are all going to die; in a very real sense, we are all terminal. We just like to push it away, far, far away; we specialize in denial, right until the possibility of death stands suddenly before us.

The old story of the donkey whose attention could only be gotten with a 2x4 is true of most of us. We hurry through life, hustling everything we can, with very little regard for the meaningful issues, for the deeper relationships, for the intimacy of love, right until we are hit by the 2x4—our own mortality.

Oregon Senator Richard Neuberger, shortly after he learned he was to die from cancer, wrote: "For the first time I think I actually am savoring life. I realize, finally, that I am not immortal. I shudder when I remember all the occasions that I spoiled for myself—even when I was in the best of health—by false pride, synthetic values, and fancied slights." Such beautiful self-awareness!

Psychologists tell us that no one can continually dwell on his or her own demise. There is a difference between morbidity and mortality. To keep before one's self the brevity of life is to enhance and enrich daily living. To dwell on one's death is to bring gloom and depression. The first is an affirmation of faith, the second is a negation of faith.

The Psalmist understood mortality and the brevity of life: "The years of our life are threescore and ten, or even by reason of strength fourscore; yet their span is but toil and trouble; they are soon gone, and we fly away. So teach us to number our days that we may get a heart of wisdom."

It would be nice to believe that people who regularly see and deal with death might not lose sight of their own mortality. No need for the 2x4. It ain't so! Each brush with serious illness was an attention-getter for me. Each was a refocusing of values, a recommitment to what and who is important. Each was a precious reminder of what German poet Johann von Goethe said:

"Nothing is worth more than this day.

You will never relive yesterday and

tomorrow is still beyond your reach."

single-minded not narrow-minded day 24

Today I had the strong feeling that things are basically quite simple. If I could love God with all my heart, all my soul, and all my mind, I would feel a great inner freedom, great enough to embrace all that exists, great enough also to prevent little events from making me lose heart. During a few hours I felt that the presence of God was so obvious and my love for him so central that all the complexities of existence seemed to unite in one point and become very simple and clear. When my heart is undivided, my mind only concerned about God, my soul full of his love, everything comes together into one perspective and nothing remains excluded. I felt the great difference between single-mindedness and narrow-mindedness.

For the first time I sensed a real single-mindedness; my mind seemed to expand and to be able to receive endlessly more than when I feel divided and confused. When all attention is on him who is my Creator, my Redeemer, and my Sanctifier, I can see all human life—joyful as well as painful—and all of creation united in his love. Then I even wonder why I was so tormented and anxious, so guilt-ridden and restless, so hurried and impatient. All these pains seemed false pains, resulting from not seeing, not hearing, and not understanding. The real pain is the pain that I find in God, who allowed all of earth's suffering to enter into his own divine intimacy. The experience of God's presence is not void of pain. But the pain is so deep that you do not want to miss it since it is in the pain that the joy of God's presence can be tasted. This seems close to nonsense except in the sense that it is beyond sense and, therefore, hard to capture within the limits of human understanding. The experience of God's unifying presence is an experience in which the distinction between joy and pain seems to be transcended and in which the beginning of a new life is intimated.

Henri J.M. Nouwen, The Genesee Diary: Report From A Trappist Monastery

If any of you lacks wisdom, let him ask God, who gives to all men generously and without reproaching, and it will be given him. But let him ask in faith, with no doubting, for he who doubts is like a wave of the sea that is driven and tossed by the wind. For that person must not suppose that a double-minded man, unstable in all his ways, will receive anything from the Lord.

James 1:5-8

I want you to know, brethren, that what has happened to me has really served to advance the gospel, so that it has become known throughout the whole praetorian guard and to all the rest that my imprisonment is for Christ; and most of the brethren have been made confident in the Lord because of my imprisonment, and are much more bold to speak the word of God without fear.

Some indeed preach Christ from envy and rivalry, but others from goodwill. The latter do it out of love, knowing that I am put here for the defense of the gospel; the former proclaim Christ out of partisanship, not sincerely but thinking to afflict me in my imprisonment. What then? Only that in every way, whether in pretense or in truth, Christ is proclaimed; and in that I rejoice.

Yes, and I shall rejoice. For I know that through your prayers and the help of the Spirit of Jesus Christ this will turn out for my deliverance, as it is my eager expectation and hope that I shall not be at all ashamed, but that with full courage now as always Christ will be honored in my body, whether by life or by death. For to me to live is Christ, and to die is gain.

Philippians 1:12-21

day 24

How would you fill in the blank, "For me to live is _____"? What central goal or purpose is your life organized around? Would you rather be single-mindedly pursuing some other goal?

day 24

SINGLE-MINDED NOT NARROW-MINDED

Every minister is captive to people at social occasions who want to talk about religion. Often they are simply trying to relieve the guilt they feel at seeing the minister because they haven't been to church or they've done something wrong or who knows what. The conversations are usually predictable.

A young man recently converted to the faith by fundamentalist friends, tells me, "You know what Romans says, Reverend. 'If you confess with your lips that Jesus is Lord...you will be saved.'" He was an attractive young man, sincere, but very narrow-minded.

A sweet young thing of New Age Awareness persuasion wanders over to talk about harmonic convergence and various gurus, "Well, we're all searching for the same thing. All those different roads will lead to the same God." Really? She certainly wasn't narrow-minded, but it would have been difficult to put substance to what she believed.

Single-mindedness commits you to an idea (or a Person) that makes all other ideas and people fall into perspective. Narrow-mindedness is the acceptance of one idea (or one Person) to the exclusion of all others. Being single-minded makes you humble; being narrow-minded makes you arrogant.

Single-mindedness is difficult to achieve. Henri Nouwen writes of his experience while in a Trappist monastery for a brief stay. The normal complications of everyday life are not likely to be as intimidating within cloistered walls as are they are outside. We struggle within the hectic pace of our normal lives to find moments to address what it means to be single-minded.

"You shall love the Lord your God with all your heart, with all your soul, and with all your mind." Single-mindedness by Biblical definition has more to do with a personal fealty. It is not an idea that possesses us, but a Person. Being single-minded is to be less self-reliant and more God-reliant.

Paul puts the answer in focus by saying, "For me to live is Christ." Most of us have a hard time putting our lives into such focus. If asked to complete the sentence "For me to live is...," what would you say? Around what or whom does your life revolve? Having such a focus is a step toward being single-minded.

It was that focus that made Paul such a powerful force in his world. Concentrated energy! Most of us spend so much time fighting the problem that we dissipate our energy before we come up with an answer. We are double-minded, multi-minded, ambivalent, very unsure of ourselves. No wonder we are not the force for good that we would like to be. We give in to peer pressure or to material distractions so easily.

There was a popular poster that read: "Just when I knew all of life's answers, they changed all the questions." In a world full of new information and data, our minds are boggled by the possibilities. How badly we need a focus that enables us to use our energies effectively.

Single-minded! What a wonderful possibility! Free from ourselves and a force for God because we have found a focus. Take your pen in hand and fill in the blank.

For me to live is _____.

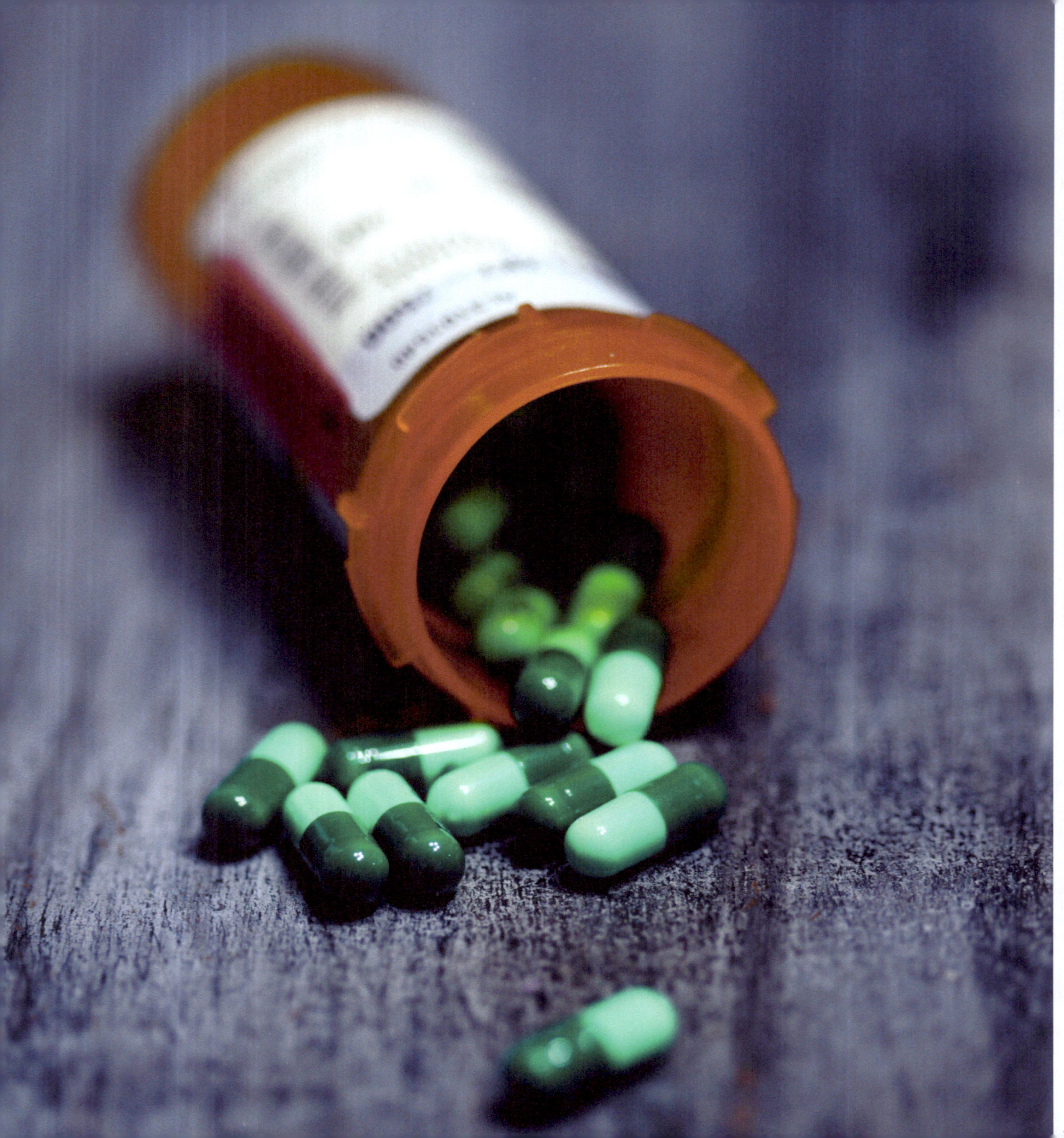

euphoric euthanasia day 25

> To be, or not to be, that is the question,
> Whether 'tis nobler in the mind to suffer
> The slings and arrows of outrageous fortune,
> Or to take arms against a sea of troubles,
> And by opposing end them? To die: to sleep;
> No more; and by a sleep to say we end
> The heart-ache and the thousand natural shocks
> That flesh is heir to, 'tis a consummation
> Devoutly to be wish'd. To die, to sleep;
> To sleep: perchance to dream: ay, there's the rub;
> For in that sleep of death what dreams may come
> When we have shuffled off this mortal coil,
> Must give us pause.
>
> *Shakespeare, Hamlet*

In our way, we conform as best we can to the rest of nature. The obituary pages tell us of the news that we are dying away, while the birth announcements in finer print, off at the side of the page, inform us of our replacements, but we get no grasp from this of the enormity of scale. There are 3 billion of us on the earth, and all 3 billion must be dead, on a schedule, within this lifetime. The vast mortality, involving something over 50 million of us each year, takes place in relative secrecy. We can only really know of the deaths in our households, or among our friends. These, detached in our minds from all the rest, we take to be unnatural events, anomalies, outrages. We speak of our own dead in low voices; struck down, we say, as though visible death can only occur for cause, by disease or violence, avoidably. We send off for flowers, grieve, make ceremonies, scatter bones, unaware of the rest of the 3 billion on the same schedule. All of that immense mass of flesh and bone and consciousness will disappear by absorption into the earth, without recognition by the transient survivors.

Less than a half century from now, our replacements will have more than doubled the numbers. It is hard to see how we can continue to keep the secret, with such multitudes doing the dying. We will have to give up the notion that death is a catastrophe, or detestable, or avoidable, or even strange. We will need to learn more about the cycling of life in the rest of the system, and about our connection to the process. Everything that comes alive seems to be in trade for something that dies, cell for cell. There might be some comfort in the recognition of synchrony, in the information that we all go down together, in the best of company.

Lewis Thomas, The Lives Of A Cell

> Man that is born of woman is of few days,
> and full of trouble.
> He comes forth like a flower, and withers;
> he flees like a shadow, and continues not.
> And dost thou open thy eyes upon such a one
> and bring him into judgment with thee?
> Who can bring a clean thing out of an unclean.
> There is only one.
> Since his days are determined,
> and the number of his months is with thee,
> and thou hast appointed his
> bounds that he cannot pass,
> Look away from him, and desist,
> that he may enjoy, like a hireling his day.
> For there is hope for a tree,
> if it be cut down that it will sprout again,
> and that its shoots will not cease.
> Though its root grow old in the earth,
> and its stump die in the ground,
> Yet at the scent of water it will bud
> and put forth branches like a young plant.
> But man dies and is laid low;

day 25

man breathes his last, and where is he?
As waters fail from a lake
and a river wastes away and dries up,
So man lies down and rises not again;
till the heavens are no more he will not awake,
or be roused out of his sleep.
Oh that thou wouldest hide me in Sheol,
that thou wouldest conceal me
until thy wrath is past,
that thou wouldest appoint a set time,
and remember me!
If a man die, shall he live again?

Job 14:1-14

It was now about the sixth hour, and there was darkness over the whole land until the ninth hour, while the sun's light failed; and the curtain of the temple was torn in two. Then Jesus, crying with a loud voice, said, "Father, into thy hands I commit my spirit! And having said this he breathed his last.

Luke 23:44-46

But we would not have you ignorant, brethren, concerning those who are asleep, that you may not grieve as others do who have no hope. For since we believe that Jesus died and rose again, even so, through Jesus, God will bring with him those who have fallen asleep. For this we declare to you by the word of the Lord, that we who are alive, who are left until the coming of the Lord, shall not precede those who have fallen asleep. For the Lord himself will descend from heaven with a cry of command, with the archangel's call, and with the sound of the trumpet of God. And the dead in Christ will rise first; then we who are alive, who are left, shall be caught up together with them in the clouds to meet the Lord in the air; and so we shall always be with the Lord. Therefore comfort one another with these words.

1 Thessalonians 4:13-18

day 25

EUPHORIC EUTHANASIA

Not too long ago a favorite lady of mine died of suicide; she was 95 years old. She failed the first time she tried. She joined The Hemlock Society, ordered their book, and read the directions for suicide. She assembled the necessary pills and took them. Unfortunately, she had been a teetotaler all her life and couldn't imagine drinking the quart of gin suggested, so her first attempt didn't work. Next time she succeeded. She didn't drink the gin but she added a plastic bag to her equipment. Rest in peace, my friend!

The only tragedy for me in her death was that no one was sympathetic with what she wanted to do. She was very old, very sick, very loving, and wanted her grandchildren to have her remaining money. She was ready to die, unafraid. But society wouldn't allow her in any legal way to end her life. She finally succeeded but with great anguish and harsh judgment from those about her.

Our society is hell-bent on keeping people alive. The desire of the person to live or the quality of life of that person are totally ignored. We condemn people to live because to choose death seems unnatural and immoral. Death is a taboo!

It follows that euthanasia is a perpetually hot topic. Euthanasia is usually defined as "mercy killing," though a more accurate rendering of the Greek is "easy death" (Merriam-Webster). It is easy to understand the controversy that the topic engenders; it is dangerous for any of us, even the wisest, to make decisions about life and death.

It is another matter, however, if a person because of age or sickness or suffering reaches a point where he or she wants to die. What's wrong with that? Why couldn't we have a committee of a doctor, lawyer, and minister who would consider the reasons with the person and, if there seemed to be justification, allow the person the necessary medication to take her own life?

There are no easy answers to the momentous problems of life and death, but it is tragic that we cannot even discuss the matter freely because of authoritarian positions taken by the church and consequent legal positions taken by our society, a society that mostly denies death.

Why do we make people go through untold physical pain and suffering, as well as mental anguish, all because of our own fears and rigidities? Who among us speaks for God? Unfortunately, a lot of people among us speak for God—the Pope, the church, many pastors, and a lot of people who claim to know God's will.

Because of antibiotics, pneumonia is no longer the "old person's friend". Hospitals and doctors don't let people die easily anymore. They're afraid of being sued. I remember an 85-year-old lady with one leg amputated and riddled with cancer who was subjected to a Code Blue (all the extraordinary means of keeping people alive when their heart stops). Why? Because we don't like dealing with death—any life is better than death. Thus, we are kinder to animals than to humans.

there is hope in a burp day 26

Now the whole earth had one language and few words. And as men migrated from the east, they found a plain in the land of Shinar and settled there. And they said to one another, "Come, let us make bricks, and burn them thoroughly." And they had brick for stone, and bitumen for mortar. Then they said, "Come, let us build ourselves a city, and a tower with its top in the heavens, and let us make a name for ourselves, lest we be scattered abroad upon the face of the whole earth."

And the Lord came down to see the city and the tower, which the sons of men had built. And the Lord said, "Behold, they are one people, and they have all one language; and this is only the beginning of what they will do; and nothing that they propose to do will now be impossible for them. Come, let us go down, and there confuse their language, that they may not understand one another's speech."

So the Lord scattered them abroad from there over the face of all the earth, and they left off building the city. Therefore, its name was called Babel, because there the Lord confused the language of all the earth; and from there the Lord scattered them abroad over all the face of the earth.

Genesis 11:1-9

When pride comes, then comes disgrace;
but with the humble is wisdom.
The integrity of the upright guides them,
but the crookedness of the treacherous destroys them
Riches do not profit in the day of wrath,
but righteousness delivers from death.

Proverbs 11:2-4

For the Lord of hosts has a day
against all that is proud and lofty,
against all that is lifted up and high;
against all the cedars of Lebanon,
lofty and lifted up;
and against all the oaks of Bashan;
against all the high mountains,
and against all the lofty hills;
against every high tower,
and against every fortified wall;
against all the ships of Tarshish,
and against all the beautiful craft.
And the haughtiness of man shall be humbled,
and the pride of men shall be brought low;
and the Lord alone will be exalted in that day.

Isaiah 2:12-17

For Jews demand signs and Greeks seek wisdom, but we preach Christ crucified, a stumbling block to Jews and folly to Gentiles, but to those who are called, both Jews and Greeks, Christ the power of God and the wisdom of God. For the foolishness of God is wiser than men, and the weakness of God is stronger than men.

For consider your call, brethren; not many of you were wise according to worldly standards, not many were powerful, not many were of noble birth; but God chose what is foolish in the world to shame the wise, God chose what is weak in the world to shame the strong, God chose what is low and despised in the world, even things that are not, to bring to nothing things that are, so that no human being might boast in the presence of God.

1 Corinthians 1:22-29

So if there is any encouragement in Christ, any incentive of love, any participation in the Spirit, any affection and sympathy, complete my joy by being of the same mind, having the same love, being in full accord and of one mind. Do nothing from selfishness or conceit, but in humility count others better than yourselves. Let each of you look not only to his own interests, but also to the interests of others. Have this mind among yourselves, which you have in Christ Jesus, who,

day 26

though he was in the form of God, did not count equality with God a thing to be grasped, but emptied himself, taking the form of a servant, being born in the likeness of men. And being found in human form he humbled himself and became obedient unto death, even death on a cross. Therefore God has highly exalted him and bestowed on him the name which is above every name, that at the name of Jesus every knee should bow, in heaven and on earth and under the earth, and every tongue confess that Jesus Christ is Lord, to the glory of God the Father.

Philippians 2:1-11

Let the lowly brother boast in his exaltation, and the rich in his humiliation, because like the flower of the grass he will pass away. For the sun rises with its scorching heat and withers the grass; its flower falls, and its beauty perishes. So will the rich man fade away in the midst of his pursuits.

James 1:9-11

Are modern people guilty of the same overreaching pride that God punished in the Tower of Babel story? Do we sometimes take ourselves and our technological accomplishments too seriously?

day 26

THERE IS HOPE IN A BURP

Every time I visit Palm Springs I am reminded of Yertle the Turtle. The desire to be higher and better has run amok! Developers build homes bigger and better, but what is worse, they build them higher and higher, slowly but surely breaking down zoning regulations, despoiling the landscape even more and making a mockery of common sense. They keep "piling up turtles" so that finally the one who buys the home at the top can say:

"I'm Yertle the Turtle! Oh, marvelous me!

For I am the ruler of all that I see."

Palm Springs, unfortunately, has no monopoly on those who want to be higher and better. That marvelous human trait seems plentiful today, even ubiquitous. Everything written about so-called "Yuppies" in the last decade places them at the forefront of those who would outdo Yertle. "Pile up those turtles."

Humility has never been a popular virtue. Almost no one I know believes Jesus when he said, "The meek shall inherit the earth." The response of most men to those words is, "Bulls___!" Humility and meekness only set one up to be a doormat. Discussions of humility, meekness, egalitarianism, and sharing based on some concept of New Testament love seem laughable.

Thank God for the burps of life that shake the mighty from their throne. As in the Yertle story, there appear to be a growing number of little turtles named Mack who simply have had enough. They are no longer willing to be weighed down by it all. They burp! And the pile of turtles, with Yertle perched on top, wobbles precariously.

There is hope in a burp. I like that idea! The Yertles of the world who have lost their sense of perspective and their sense of humor need to hear more burps. The proud and greedy of our day need to hear more burps; they need to have our help in understanding that they are laughable.

It didn't take God long to catch on to our grandiose schemes. Hellbent on taking over the highest points of land and constructing the highest building possible, they wanted to be up there with God. Why should God have all the glory? "Come, let us build ourselves a city, and a tower with its top in the heavens, and let us make a name for ourselves..." Stack up those turtles.

But God burped and we've never recovered. We keep trying. We keep reaching up higher and higher, pretending we're better and better, stacking up those turtles. Hey, look at us. Aren't we something? Aren't we better than all those below?

I'm king of the hill! I'm heading the merger!

I'll do what it takes, the truth I will perjure!

My house will be better! My possessions the best!

I don't give a damn about all of the rest!

The best is for us, so much for the rabble,

We'll call our new place The Tower of Babel.

There is hope in a burp. Will God burp again? Will we? Will the Macks of the world rise up and unite? Stay tuned!

dealing with the absurd day 27

"You're wasting your time," Doc Daneeka was forced to tell him.

"Can't you ground someone who's crazy?"

"Oh, sure. I have to. There's a rule saying I have to ground anyone who's crazy."

"Then why don't you ground me. I'm crazy. Ask Clevinger"

"Clevinger? Where is Clevinger? You find Clevinger and I'll ask him."

"Then ask any of the others. They'll tell you crazy I am."

"They're crazy."

"Then why don't you ground them?"

"Why don't they ask me to ground them?"

"Because they're crazy, that's why."

"Of course they're crazy," Doc Daneeka replied. "I just told you they're crazy, didn't I? And you can't let crazy people decide whether you're crazy or not, can you?"

Yossarian looked at him soberly and tried another approach. "Is Orr crazy?"

"He sure is," Doc Daneeka said.

"Can you ground him?"

"I sure can. But first he has to ask me to. That's part of the rule."

"Then why doesn't he ask you to?"

"Because he's crazy," Doc Daneeka said. "He has to be crazy to keep flying combat missions after all the close calls he's had. Sure I can ground Orr. But first he has to ask me."

"That's all he has to do to be grounded."

"That's all. Let him ask me."

"And then you can ground him?" Yossarian asked?

"No. Then I can't ground him."

"You mean there's a catch."

"Sure there's a catch." Doc Daneeka replied. "Catch 22. Anyone who wants to get out of combat duty isn't really crazy."

There was only one catch and that was Catch 22, which specified that a concern for one's safety in the face of dangers that were real and immediate was the process of a rational mind. Orr was crazy and could be grounded. All he had to do was ask; and as soon as he did, he would no longer be crazy and would have to fly more missions. Orr would be crazy to fly more missions and sane if he didn't, but if he was sane he had to fly them. If he flew them he was crazy and didn't have to; but if he didn't want to he was sane and had to. Yossarian was moved very deeply by the absolute simplicity of this clause of Catch 22 and let out a respectful whistle.

"That's some catch, that Catch 22," he observed.

"It's the best there is," Doc Daneeka agreed.

Joseph Heller, Catch 22

The dinosaurs disappeared not because they were too weak, but because they were too strong. Their fantastic power came from a biological framework which was basically absurd, and the result was annihilation. Can you cure an insane person by making his body physically fit? Obviously not. This would add power to insanity, making it more insane still. The power generated by an irrational structure only tends to aggravate the very irrationality from which it springs. By adding power to the absurd one does not abolish it; on the contrary, it becomes still more hopelessly entangled in itself...

Our civilization is behaving just like the dinosaur. Underneath everything it does, one finds the ultimate certainty that there is no problem that cannot be solved by means of a little more power. It is not by accident that for years detergent makers have been advertising "stronger," "faster," "more concentrated" and improved formulas. They know that these values control our collective unconscious. What is stronger must be better. Love of power has become our obsession, and power itself our sole god...

The same is true of the logic of war. It has a single purpose: power, sheer power. This is one of the shocking revelations of the Pentagon Papers. There they are, the professionals of

day 27

war! Their eyes and minds are turned to a situation which is filled with suffering, death, and despair. But they do not feel the suffering. They do not mention the corpses. They do not see the despair. As with the economy, the logic of war is concerned only with a systemic result: the increase of power. If love of power becomes the ultimate concern of a system, all questions about values must be dropped. Power becomes more important than life, while life is reduced to a mere means of power. Then the only questions raised are where, when, and how to exercise power.

This is how the dinosaur operated. His logic was remarkably similar to that of modern pragmatism. Both in effect keep repeating: "I need not worry about the whole—the whole will take care of itself." One takes for granted the basic structure and moves on to develop its size, power, and efficacy to the utmost limits. If something does not function well, it is because the system has not increased its power to the proper level at that point. Like the dinosaur, we ignore the fact that if the basic system is irrational and structurally faulty, greater power only accentuates its weakness. As a strong insane man is more dangerous than a weak one, the increase of power in a sick system can only produce unexpected forms of its own derangement and eventually its downfall.

The fundamental question of values is never raised. We refuse to criticize the foundations upon which our civilization is built, because we simply assume that they are right. We do not want to become radicals...to go to the root of things.

Rubem Alves, Tomorrow's Child

"But I don't want to go among mad people," Alice remarked.

"Oh, you can't help that," said the Cat: "we're all mad here. I'm mad. You're mad."

"How do you know I'm mad?" said Alice.

"You must be," said the Cat, "or you wouldn't have come here."

Lewis Carroll, Alice in Wonderland

"The first thing is not to despair. Men must never give in to the absurdity of life, must in fact, fight it continuously as a condition of life. Man cannot be written off so long as he fights whatever is evil. He may have to fight continuously but the fight justifies his existence.

Albert Camus, The Plague

In the world you have tribulation but be of good cheer, I have overcome the world.

John 16:31

How does your sense of humor function when nothing makes any sense? Can a faith perspective help you laugh at the absurdity of life and take the nonsense in stride?

day 27

DEALING WITH THE ABSURD

"Absurd: ridiculously unreasonable, unsound, or incongruous, having no rational or orderly relationship to man's life." So says Webster's New Collegiate Dictionary, but it doesn't take a dictionary definition to tell us that there is an awful lot about life today that is absurd.

Joseph Heller could hardly have foreseen our world when he wrote Catch 22 in 1952, but for many his book seems prescient, even prophetic, filled with insight into a world yet to come. Like Yossarian in Heller's book, we recognize the absurd nature of the world and would like to escape it, but if we are clearheaded enough to recognize the absurdity, then we have no excuse and we must stay and deal with it. "That is some catch, Catch 22."

Trying to be rational in an irrational world leaves us with a feeling of the absurd. Popular slogans speak of the absurd:

"The hurrier I go, the behinder I get."

"The harder I try, the worse it gets."

"Cheer up! Things could be worse! And so he cheered up... and things got worse."

"Some things change, some things never change."

"The more things change, the more they stay the same."

We who live in America are the most fortunate of all people, but most of us know the absurdity of trying to deal with federal agencies. SNAFU (Situation Normal All Fouled Up—yes, I know that is the polite way of saying it) is the order of the day once you get afoul of a government employee or, God help you, a computer that keeps sending the same non-sensical message to you long after you have run out of ideas for how to extract useful information. Even for a church to build a new structure on its own property may require dealing with as many as twenty-seven different state agencies. Ridiculous? Absurd!

Both those who control the social-welfare system and average Americans want people to get off "the dole"; indeed, most people on the dole would love nothing more than to have a job and the salary and dignity that come with it. But we seldom examine the system. We profess that we want to keep families together, but as soon as a man goes to live with a single mother and her children, the welfare stops, which only encourages the couple to live separately. Entry-level jobs that begin to help people make it on their own usually bring a corresponding and immediate cut in welfare, taking parents away from their kids without increasing income. Self-defeating? You bet! Absurdity in our social-welfare system is easy to chronicle.

Absurdity is everywhere, even in the church. We are now out to save the world by taking a stance on every social problem and political issue as though we really knew the answers. That we have Biblical insight, energy, and input is important, but that we have the answers and always know better than others is absurd.

Faith helps us to be rational in an irrational world, to keep our sense of humor amidst the absurdity around us. We struggle against the Catch 22's of the world, "the powers of darkness," as we look once again to a God who brought cosmos out of chaos, light out of darkness, and love out of hate—who transmuted the ugliness of the cross into something that was and is beautiful in its redemptive powers

Jesus said, "In the world you have tribulation, but be of good cheer, I have overcome the world," even the absurd world.

new ways of seeing day 28

Again on the road, I drove up a lumpy, dry plateau, all the while thinking of the errors that had led me to Hat Creek. The word error comes from a Middle English word, erren, which means "to wander about," as in the knight errant. The word evolved to mean "going astray" and that evolved to mean "mistake." As for mistake, it derives from Old Norse and once meant "to take wrongly." Yesterday, I had been mistaken and in error, taking one wrong road after another. As a result, I had come to a place of clear beauty and met a man who carried his philosophy on a cafe-business card.

The annals of scientific discovery are full of errors that opened new worlds: Bell was working on an apparatus to aid the deaf when he invented the telephone; Edison was tinkering with the telephone when he invented the phonograph. If a man can keep alert and imaginative, an error is a possibility, a chance at something new; to him wandering and wondering are part of the same process, and he is most mistaken, most in error, whenever he quits exploring.

The Boss of the Plains had said (after he mentioned his death wish) that his life had come to seem more and more of the same thing, and he called the story of his life Ten Thousand Mistakes. It stood to reason. To him a mistake was deviation from preconceived ideas, from standard answers, from wandering off the marked route. To him, change meant error.

Biochemists hold that evolution proceeds by random genetic changes—errors—and that each living thing is an experiment within the continuum of trial and error and temporary success. In nature, correct means harmony that breeds survival. Always to demand established routes, habitual ways, then, is to go against the grain of life; that is often the Indian impulse. But to engage in the continuing experiment is to reach for harmony. Hesse writes:

"I am an experiment on the part of nature, a gamble within the unknown, perhaps for a new purpose, perhaps for nothing, and my only task is to allow this game on the part of the primeval depths to take its course, to feel its will within me and make it wholly mine."

Whitman said it too, "A man is a summons and a challenge."

William Least Heat Moon,
Blue Highways (A Journey Into America)

Had I gone looking for some particular place rather than any place, I'd never have found this spring under the sycamores. Since leaving home, I felt for the first time at rest. Sitting full in the moment, I practiced on the god-awful difficulty of just paying attention. It's a contention of Heat Moon's—believing as he does any traveler who misses the journey misses about all he's going to get—that a man becomes his attentions. His observations and curiosity, they make and remake him.

Etymology: curious, related to cure, once meant "carefully observant." Maybe a tonic of curiosity would counter my numbing sense that life inevitably creeps toward the absurd. Absurd, by the way, derives from a Latin word meaning "deaf, dulled." Maybe the road could provide a therapy through observation of the ordinary and obvious, a means whereby the outer eye opens an inner eye. STOP, LOOK, LISTEN, the old railroad crossing signs warned. Whitman calls it, "the profound lesson of reception."

New ways of seeing can disclose new things: the radio telescope revealed quasars and pulsars, and the scanning electron microscope showed the whiskers of the dust mite. But turn the question around: Do new things make for new ways of seeing?

William Least Heat Moon,
Blue Highways (A Journey Into America)

day 28

Then the disciples of John came to him saying, "Why do we and the Pharisees fast, but your disciples do not fast?" And Jesus said to them," Can the wedding guests mourn as long as the bridegroom is with them? The days will come, when the bridegroom is taken away from them, and then they will fast. And no one puts a piece of unshrunk cloth on an old garment, for the patch tears away from the garment, and a worse tear is made. Neither is new wine put into old wineskins; if it is, the skins burst, and the wine is spilled, and the skins are destroyed; but new wine is put into fresh wineskins, and so both are preserved."

Matthew 9:14-17

And he who sat upon the throne said, "Behold, I make all things new." Also he said, "Write this, for these words are trustworthy and true." And he said to me. "It is done! I am the Alpha and the Omega, the beginning and the end.

Revelation 21:5-6

From now on, therefore, we regard no one from a human point of view; even though we once regarded Christ from a human point of view, we regard him thus no longer. Therefore, if any one is in Christ, he is a new creation; the old has passed away, behold, the new has come. All this is from God, who through Christ reconciled us to himself and gave us the ministry of reconciliation; that is, God was in Christ reconciling the world to himself, not counting their trespasses against them, and entrusting to us the message of reconciliation. So we are ambassadors for Christ, God making his appeal through us. We beseech you on behalf of Christ, be reconciled to God.

II Corinthians 5:16-20

day 28

NEW WAYS OF SEEING

For some time now I have been wearing progressive trifocals. They are better for golf because my view of the ball doesn't get lost in the lines between the various lenses. At the beginning, they confused me like crazy, though I am finally adjusting. In fact, now I would be lost without them. My sight has become used to and dependent upon those lenses.

In some ways that's an analogy for life. After a certain length of time we develop lenses through which we see the various people and relationships that compose our lives. We become so used to those lenses that it is hard to manage without them. It becomes very difficult to see anything in a new way, especially those people close to us, because of that highly developed set of lenses reflecting thoughts, emotions, words, and nonverbal communication over many years. If a relationship breaks down and we seek some therapeutic assistance, the therapist must break those lenses so that we can see things differently.

One of a minister's most difficult jobs is attempting to get people to see life in a different way. The New Testament gives us the words of Jesus which contain values quite contrary, even topsy-turvy, to our world. Phrases such as:

"Blessed are the meek for they shall inherit the earth." WHO??

"If anyone strikes you on the right cheek, turn to him the other also." YOU'RE KIDDING!!

"The last shall be first and the first shall be last." WRONG!!

"He who would be the greatest among you must be the servant of all." THIS MAN HAS FLIPPED.

"He who saves his life shall lose it and he who loses his life for my sake and the gospel's shall save it." RIGHT!!!

Seeing the world as Jesus might adds a different perspective. Those highly developed lenses through which we have seen life and understood our relationships for so long must be broken. Dashed to pieces! "From now on we regard no one from a human point of view." That's the perspective of faith, a new way of seeing.

Trifocals are one way of seeing things anew; faith is yet another. The question remains, however: is that something we want? Whether we wear glasses or not, the lenses we have developed through which we view the world and our relationships are very comfortable. Seeing things anew often challenges old and comfortable ways. Why do that? Change, in whatever form it comes, is greatly resisted by humans.

Like William Least Heat Moon in his journeys, we often learn the most when we make a mistake. We err and go down the wrong path and we are then forced to see things differently. After the fact we may think the error was providential. It is sad that we see things anew more in retrospect than in prospect. Faith should lead us to risk more, to be more curious ("carefully observant").

If it is God who "makes all things new," then faith calls us to break our comfortable old lenses. Dash them to bits! Yes, get rid of those old "rose-colored glasses" and try the lenses that Jesus urges. Different, challenging, exciting—all possibilities for a new way of seeing.

strangers and sojourners **day 29**

The true West differs from the East in one great, pervasive, influential, and awesome way: space. The vast openness changes the roads, towns, houses, farms, crops, machinery, politics, economics, and, naturally, ways of thinking. How could it do otherwise? Space west of the line is perceptible and often palpable, especially when it appears empty, and it's that apparent emptiness which makes matter look alone, exiled, and unconnected. Those spaces diminish man and reduce his blindness to the immensity of the universe; they push him toward a greater reliance on himself, and, at the same time, to a greater awareness of others and what they do. But as the space diminishes man and his constructions in a material fashion, it also—paradoxically—makes them more noticeable. Things show up out here. No one, not even the sojourner, escapes the expanses. You can't get away from them by rolling up the safety-glass and speeding through, because the terrible distances eat up speed. Even dawn takes nearly an hour just to cross Texas. Still, drivers race along: but when you get down to it, they are people uneasy about space...

A car whipped past, the driver eating and a passenger clicking a camera. Moving without going anywhere, taking a trip instead of making one. I laughed at the absurdity of the photographs and then realized I, too, was rolling effortlessly along, turning the windshield into a movie screen in which I, the viewer, did the moving while the subject held still. That was the temptation of the American highway, of the American vacation (from the Latin word vacare, "to be empty"). A woman in Texas had told me that she often threatened to write a book about her family vacations. Her title: Zoom! The drama of their trips, she said, occurred on the inside of the windshield with one family crisis after another. Her husband drove a thousand miles, much of it with his right arm over the backseat to hold down one of the children. She said, "Our vacations take us."

She longed for the true journey of an Odysseus or Ishmael or Gulliver or even a Dorothy of Kansas, wherein passage through space and time becomes only a metaphor of a movement through the interior of being. A true journey, no matter how long the travel takes, has no end. What's more, as John Le Carre, in speaking of the journey of death, said, "Nothing ever bridged the gulf between the man who went and the man who stayed."

William Least Heat Moon, Blue Highways (A Journey Into America)

O to realize space!
The plenteousness of all, that
there are no bounds,
To emerge and be of the sky, of
the sun and moon and
flying clouds,
as one with them.

Walt Whitman, A Song of Joys

I had an obsession with the Amish. Plain and simple. Objectively it made no sense. I, who worked hard at being special, fell in love with a people who valued being ordinary.

When I told people I wanted to live with an Amish family everybody laughed. "Impossible," they said. "No Amish family will take you in."

I didn't know when I first looked at an Amish quilt and felt my heart pounding that my soul was starving, that an inner voice was trying to make sense of my life.

I didn't know that I was beginning a journey of the spirit, what Carlos Castenada calls following "a path that has heart."

I thought I was going to learn more about their quilts, but the quilts were only guides, leading me to what I really needed to learn, to answer a question I hadn't formed yet:

"Is there another way to lead a good life?"

day 29

I went searching in a foreign land and found my way home.

Perhaps each of us has a starved place, and each of us knows deep down what we need to fill that place. To find the courage to trust and honor the search, to follow the voice that tells us what we need to do, even when it doesn't seem to make sense, is a worthy pursuit. This story is about that search.

Maybe you have a dream, incubating, not fully formed. Maybe you are on a similar quest. I hope you will listen to my story and at the same time hear yours. That way it will be our journey.

Sue Bender, Plain And Simple

I'm just a poor, wayfaring stranger,
A trav'ling through this world of woe;
But there's no sickness, no toil or danger,
In that bright world to which I go.

I'm going there to see my mother,
I'm going there, no more to roam,
I'm just a-going over Jordan,
I'm just a-going over home

Traditional American Folk Hymn

These all died in faith, not having received what was promised, but having seen it and greeted it from afar, and having acknowledged that they were strangers and exiles on the earth. For people who speak thus make it clear that they are seeking a homeland. If they had been thinking of that land from which they had gone out, they would have had opportunity to return. But as it is, they desire a better country, that is, a heavenly one. Therefore god is not ashamed to be called their God, for he has prepared for them a city.

Hebrews 11:13-16

day 29

STRANGERS AND SOJOURNERS

Some people love to travel. Retirement brings great joy to them because for the first time they can go whenever they want. The underlying assumption, of course, is home. They love to see new things and new places, but "there's no place like home." They don't mind being in a strange land for a while but when all is said and done, there is no greater joy than being homeward bound.

To be a stranger all the time would be unbearable. The plight of "the homeless" in America is so poignant because most of us cannot fathom what it would be like to be without a home. We have memorized and rehearsed the sayings about home:

"Home is where the heart is." (Pliny)

"Stay, stay at home, my heart, and rest;

Home-keeping hearts are happiest." (Longfellow)

"A man travels the world over in search of what he needs, and then returns home to find it."

Home represents the continuities of our lives. Significant people, special places, and lasting memories are all tied up there. People are supposed to know us and recognize us when we are home. They know who we are; we are not strangers. How many times have you been home in your life?

The Gospel of John records that after the crucifixion, "the disciples went home again." We understand! What we don't understand and don't want to hear is the Bible telling us we are "strangers and sojourners." This earth is not our home. We are just poor wayfaring strangers. Whoa! Hold on there! What kind of nonsense is that?

Israel was promised a land of their own so they would no longer be strangers and sojourners, and they are still fighting for it today. So are their Palestinian neighbors. We understand that because we also love our homeland and would fight for it; it is our land. We don't mind temporarily being a stranger in someone else's land, but not in our own land. This is home! It's ours! Mine!

Faith, at times, seems more unsettling than settling. Whose earth is it anyway? The Psalmist made that clear:

"The earth is the Lord's and the fullness thereof,

The people and they that dwell therein." (Psalm 24:1)

When our ownership of the earth is self-centered, trouble begins. History is a clear record of those troubles.

Our homeless might relate to the perspective of that old folk song, "I'm just a poor wayfaring stranger, travelin' through this world of woe." But most of us have a strong sense of home. So we are unable to identify with the plight of the homeless even though their problems hold a poignancy for us. But they have something to teach us.

God may have "prepared for us a city," but that has to wait until the time comes. For now, this is our home, with its wars and rumors of wars, its troubles and disruptions. In some sense, we are all strangers and sojourners in this life, no matter how hard we work to make a home here.

Unsettling faith again—life is a journey no matter where we live. We are all strangers and sojourners. And when we come down to that final moment of life, whether we are dying in a hospital, convalescent home, or our own home, what will matter is an eternal home. "The eternal God is our dwelling place, and underneath are his everlasting arms." That's home to us strangers!

the human being awaits a besieger **day 30**

If I have anything to say worth saying on the subject of human values, I owe most of it to her. The Siege is the story of the first eight years of the life of Clara Park's autistic daughter. In the book the daughter is called Elly. It is a book about a particular autistic child and her family. And it is also, indirectly, a book about people in general and their search for meaning. We are still quite ignorant of the nature and causes of autism, but we know at least this much. The autistic child is deficient in those mental faculties which enable us to attach meaning to our experiences. We all from time to time have difficulty in grasping the meanings of things which happen to us. The autistic child has the same difficulty in an extreme degree. The siege by which Clara and her husband and her three older children battered their way into Elly's mind was only an extreme case of the struggle which all teachers must wage to reach the minds of their pupils. The task is the same, to bring a sense of the meaning of life to minds which have lost an awareness of meaning or never possessed it… Clara is telling us that the search for human values is a two-sided thing. We must be borrowers as well as lenders. The measure of Clara's achievement is that she not only planted in Elly's meaningless solitude an understanding of the meaning of human contact and conversation, but also distilled out of Elly's illness insights which gave added meaning to her own life, to the life of her family, and to her work as a teacher… Here is her own summing up, describing how a teacher is ready to receive as well as to give meaning.

I learn from Elly and I learn from my students; they also teach me about Elly. In the early years, I knew a student who was himself emerging from a dark citadel; he had been to Menninger Clinic and to other places too, and he knew from inside the ways of thought I had to learn. "Things get too much for her and she just turns down the volume," he told me. I remember that, because I have seen it so often since, in Elly and in so many others. Human beings fortify themselves in many ways. Numbness, weakness, irony, inattention, silence, suspicion are only a few of the materials out of which the personality constructs its walls. With experience gained in my siege of Elly I mount smaller sieges. Each one is undertaken with hesitation; to try to help anyone is an arrogance. But Elly is there to remind me that to fail to try is a dereliction. Not all my sieges are successful. But where I fail, I have learned that I fail because of my own clumsiness and inadequacy, not because the enterprise is impossible. However formidable the fortifications, they can be breached. I have not found one person, however remote, however hostile, who did not wish for what he seemed to fight. Of all the things that Elly has given, the most precious is this faith, a faith experience has almost transformed into certain knowledge: that inside the strongest citadel he can construct. the human being awaits his besieger.

Freeman Dyson, Weapons And Hope

I fled him, down the nights and down the days;
I fled him, down the arches of the years;
I fled him, down the labyrinthine ways
Of my own mind; and in the midst of tears
I hid from him, and under running laughter.
Up vistaed hopes I sped
And shot, precipitated,
Adown Titanic glooms of chasmed fears,
From those strong Feet that
followed, followed after.
But with unhurrying chase,
And unperturbed pace,
Deliberate speed, majestic instancy,
They beat—and a Voice beat
More instant than the Feet—
"All things betray thee, who betrayest Me."
I pleaded, outlaw-wise,
By many a hearted casement, curtained red,
Trellised with intertwining charities;
(For, though I knew His love who followed,
Yet was I sore adread
Lest having him, I must have naught beside);
But, if one little casement parted wide,

day 30

The gust of His approach would clash to it.
Fear wist not to evade, as Love wist to pursue

* * * * *

Now of that long pursuit
Comes at hand the Bruit;
That voice is round me like a bursting sea:
"And is thy earth so marred,
Shattered in shard on shard?
Lo, all things fly thee, for thou fliest Me!
Strange, piteous, futile thing!
Wherefore should any set thee love apart?
Seeing none but I make much
of draught" (He said),
"And human love needs human meriting:
How hast thou merited—
Of all man's clotted clay the dingiest clot?
Alack, thou knowest not
How little worthy of any love thou art!
Whom wilt thou find to love ignoble thee
Save Me, save only Me?
All which I took from thee I did but take
Not for thy harms,
But just that thou might'st seek it in My arms.
All which thy child's mistake
Fancies as lost, I have stored for thee at home:
Rise, clasp My hand, and come!"
Halts by me that footfall:
Is my gloom, after all,
Shade of His hand, outstretched caressingly?
"Ah, fondest, blindest, weakest,
I am He whom thou seekest!
Thou dravest love from thee, who dravest Me."

Francis Thompson, The Hound of Heaven

While we were still weak, at the right time Christ died for the ungodly. Why, one will hardly die for a righteous man—though perhaps for a good man one will dare even to die. But God shows his love for us in that while we were yet sinners Christ died for us. Since, therefore, we are now justified by his blood, much more shall we be saved by him from the wrath of God. For if while we were enemies we were reconciled to God by the death of his Son, much more, now that we are reconciled, shall we be saved by his life. Not only so, but we also rejoice in God through our Lord Jesus Christ, through whom we have now received our reconciliation.

Romans 5:6-11

Are there areas of life where you've confined yourself in a protective citadel? Can you allow yourself to be open and vulnerable? Do you know others who live in protective citadels? How can you help to lay siege to the citadel imprisoning someone you know?

day 30

THE HUMAN BEING AWAITS A BESIEGER

I know a man who hates me. It's an unpleasant reality in my life, but it is true. His reasons for such intensity of feeling, imagined or real, true or false, seem not to matter, for neither appeals to rationality nor attempts to communicate have helped. I was and am the evil one and he hates me. His daughter said at the time, "You have never seen one of my father's mads."

She was right! Eight years later he is still mad. He once thought I was a good guy, even a good preacher. No more! Whenever we meet, he grunts or glowers or ignores me. If looks could kill, they could have tried him for murder long before now.

It is frightening to see the force of such hate, "his mad" as his daughter referred to it. It isolates him not only from me but from many others.

From across the years I recall two women who became well known for their eccentricities and inability to cope with the world. One was a brilliant student in college but had a nervous breakdown and never recovered. The other was a slightly confused adult who suffered from lack of guidance and lack of support from her parents who were obviously embarrassed by her deficiencies.

Only with the most painful effort could either one of them be reached by others who wanted to help. Their citadels of confusion and despair resisted even the most caring.

Siege is the appropriate word for the attempt to reach such persons, but sieges are hard to come by these days. People don't have time and patience grows thin. Rebuff after rebuff sours compassion and brings fatigue. Shortly, those who would help grow calloused and wall themselves off. Their vulnerability is too great. How difficult it is to mount a siege on a seemingly impregnable fortress.

There is great hope in Clara Park's writing, but it is oh so hard. It would seem to take a love on a par with God's love—AGAPE: unconquerable benevolence, invincible good will. Most of us just aren't that loving when our vulnerability is threatened.

Reaching out to others even when they are desirable persons to befriend is not always easy, but finding the reserves deep down inside ourselves to continue battering away at the impregnable walls built by those less desirable to befriend takes every bit of faith that we have.

"To try to help anyone is an arrogance... but to fail to try is a dereliction"—a marvelous statement and an unbelievable challenge. Working with people, especially those who have built citadels around themselves, takes as much competence and compassion as any of us can muster. When all else fails, try, try again. Not to try is a dereliction.

I am bothered by the man who hates me, but I am also buoyed by the possibility that inside that unbelievable citadel he has built, he awaits his besieger. Reconciliation for such a person can only come from a God who doesn't quit. Jesus never did! Try, try again! And so there was a cross. You and I, too, rejoice in that cross and in our reconciliation.

Thanks be to God!

the great roles are prosaic day 31

A time like this is not comfortable, secure, lazy. It is a time when tides of history over which he has no control sweep over the individual. It is a time of agony, of peril, of suffering—an ugly, hateful, cruel, brutish time at best. It is a time of war, of mass slaughter, of depravity, of mockery of all laws of God or man. It is a time in which no one can take for granted the world he lives in, the things he treasures, or the values and principles that seem to him so obvious. Those of us who have been spared the horrors in which our age specializes, who have never suffered total war, slave-labor camp or police terror, not only owe thanks; we owe charity and compassion.

But ours is also a time of new vision and greatness, of opportunity and challenge, to everyone in his daily life, as a person and as a citizen. It is a time in which everyone is an understudy to the leading role in the drama of human destiny. Everyone must be ready to take over alone and without notice, and show himself saint or hero, villain or coward. On this stage the great roles are not written in the iambic pentameter or the Alexandrine of the heroic theater. They are prosaic—played out in one's daily life, in one's work, in one's citizenship, in one's compassion or lack of it, in one's courage to stick to an unpopular principle, and in one's refusal to sanction man's inhumanity to man in an age of cruelty and moral numbness.

In a time of change and challenge, new vision and new danger, new frontiers and permanent crisis, suffering and achievement, in a time of overlap such as ours, the individual is both all-powerless and all-powerful. He is powerless, however exalted his station, if he believes that he can impose his will, that he can command the tides of history. He is all-powerful, no matter how lowly, if he knows himself to be responsible.

Peter F. Drucker, Landmarks Of Tomorrow

I am only one,
but I am one.
I cannot do everything,
but I can do something.
What I can do,
I ought to do, and
What I ought to do,
By God's grace I will do.

Edward Everett Hale

He who is greatest among you shall be your servant; whoever exalts himself will be humbled, and whoever humbles himself will be exalted.

Matthew 23:11-12

When the Son of man comes in his glory, and all the angels with him, then he will sit on his glorious throne. Before him will be gathered all the nations, and he will separate them one from another as a shepherd separates the sheep from the goats, and he will place the sheep at his right hand, but the goats at the left. Then the King will say to those at his right hand, 'Come, O blessed of my Father, inherit the kingdom prepared for you from the foundation of the world; for I was hungry and you gave me food, I was thirsty and you gave me drink, I was a stranger and you welcomed me, I was naked and you clothed me, I was sick and you visited me, I was in prison and you came to me.' Then the righteous will answer him, 'Lord, when did we see thee hungry and feed thee, or thirsty and give thee drink? And when did we see thee a stranger and welcome thee, or naked and clothe thee? And when did we see thee sick or in prison and visit thee?' And the King will answer them, 'Truly, I say to you, as you did it to one of the least of these my brethren, you did it to me.' Then he will say to those at his left hand, 'Depart from me, you cursed, into the eternal fire prepared for the devil and his angels; for I was hungry and you gave me no food, I was thirsty and you gave me no drink, I was a stranger and

day 31

you did not welcome me, naked and you did not clothe me, sick and in prison and you did not visit me.' Then they also will answer, 'Lord, when did we see thee hungry or thirsty or a stranger or naked or sick or in prison, and did not minister to thee?' Then he will answer them, 'Truly, I say to you, as you did it not to one of the least of these, you did it not to me.' And they will go away into eternal punishment, but the righteous into eternal life."

Matthew 25:31-46

And an argument arose among them as to which of them was the greatest. But when Jesus perceived the thought of their hearts, he took a child and put him by his side, and said to them, "Whoever receives this child in my name receives me, and whoever receives me receives him who sent me; for he who is least among you all is the one who is great.

Luke 9:46-48

Do you sometimes think you need to accomplish something spectacular in order for your actions to matter? In what prosaic roles can you do something small but great today?

THE GREAT ROLES ARE PROSAIC

We have a funny problem at our church—taking up the offering. We never seem to do it right, or so our Deacons think. Four people working together can create more different patterns of offering-collecting behavior than it is possible to imagine. They never do it the same way and sometimes the results are hilarious. Actually, I think the congregation, those that are aware, rather enjoy it.

This is not an important problem, but it is an indicative problem, indicative of the change in people's time commitments. In the "good old days" we used to have the same head usher every Sunday; one man served eight consecutive years. Now we do not have the same head usher or ushers two Sundays in a row. The ushers used to be all men and they walked down the aisle like a drill team with sergeant in command, lock-step. Now it is more like a covey of young quail following their parents wondering where to go next to stay out of trouble.

It is not that people are not willing or good spirited; they are. But the problem does not seem worthy of great attention and so there is no desire to improve. Why worry about or practice something so prosaic, something that doesn't make a lot of difference in people's lives? That's a fair question.

The problem lies not in taking up the offering but in the time commitments of our lives. We tend to want to be always doing big, important things and pay very little attention to the small details of daily living. Those things that attract large segments of our time, that we attack with great intensity, often have more glamour than substance. We yearn to achieve great things.

Our new environmental concerns arise from the fact that we pay little attention to the details nearest at hand. We don't even manage our own garbage very well, we waste water and valuable resources, we don't pay attention until there is a problem.

Our children take over our lives. Their schedules are incredibly demanding of us and of them. We give our time commitments to offer them every advantage of school, athletic endeavors, special projects, you name it, but we often neglect just the simple time commitment of being with them and sharing ourselves, loving them quietly and proudly. That's too prosaic!

I agree wholeheartedly with Peter Drucker. In today's world "the great roles are not written in iambic pentameter...they are prosaic—played out in one's daily life, in one's work, in one's citizenship, in one's compassion or lack of it, in one's courage to stick to an unpopular principle."

Most of us will not create artistic masterpieces with new and bold strokes of a highly talented hand. Most of us will bring change for good in this world by the small things we do—even by the way we take up the offering. Our desire to be responsible and do the best job we can in whatever we are doing will make a difference.

It is a tough world in which to be responsible but it is our world. God calls us to be part of the answer and not part of the problem. Prosaic as they are, little things matter. Jesus said, "He who is faithful in little will be made faithful in much."

unfreakability: the art of quieting the mind day 32

Perhaps the most indispensable tool for man in modern times is the ability to remain calm in the midst of rapid and unsettling changes. The person who will best survive the present age is the one Kipling described as one who can keep his head while all about are losing theirs. "Unfreakability" refers not to man's propensity for burying his head in the sand at the sight of danger, but to the ability to see the true nature of what is happening around him and to be able to respond appropriately. This requires a mind which is clear because it is calm.

"Freaking out" is a general term used for an upset mind. For example, it describes what happens in the minds of many tennis players just after they have hit a shallow lob, or while preparing to serve on match point with the memory of past double faults rushing through their minds. Freaking out is what some stockbrokers do when the market begins to plunge; what some parents do when their child has not returned from a date on time; or what most of the human population would do if they heard that beings from outer space had landed on Earth. The mind gets so upset that it does not see clearly enough what is happening to take the appropriate action. When action is born in worry and self-doubt, it is usually inappropriate and often too late to be effective.

The causes of "freak-outs" can be grouped into three categories: regret about past events; fear or uncertainty about the future; and dislike of a present event or situation. In all cases, the event and the mind's reaction to it are two separate things. It takes both to produce the result, but the freak-out is in and of the mind; it is not an attribute of the event itself.

W. Timothy Gallwey, The Inner Game Of Tennis

If you can keep your head when all about you
Are losing theirs and blaming it on you;
If you can trust yourself when
all men doubt you,
But make allowance for their doubting too;
If you can wait and not be tired by waiting,
Or, being lied about, don't deal in lies,
Or, being hated, don't give way to hating,
And yet don't look too good, nor talk too wise;
If you can dream—and not make
dreams your master;
If you can think—and not make
thoughts your aim;
If you can meet with triumph and disaster
And treat those two imposters just the same;
If you can bear to hear the truth you've spoken
Twisted by knaves to make a trap for fools,
Or watch the things you gave your life to broken,
And stoop and build 'em up with worn out tools;
If you can make one heap of all your winnings
And risk it on one turn of pitch-and-toss,
And lose, and start again at your beginnings
And never breathe a word about your loss;
If you can force your heart and nerve and sinew
To serve your turn long after they are gone,
And so hold on when there is nothing in you
Except the Will which says to them: "Hold on";
If you can talk with crowds
and keep your virtue,
Or walk with kings—nor lose
the common touch;
If neither foes nor loving friends can hurt you;
If all men count with you, but none too much;
If you can fill the unforgiving minute
With sixty seconds' worth of distance run—
Yours is the Earth and everything that's in it,
And—which is more—you'll be a Man, my son!

Rudyard Kipling

A mighty fortress is our God,
a bulwark never failing;
Our helper He, amid the flood
of mortal ills prevailing;
For still our ancient foe doth
seek to work us woe;
His craft and power are great

day 32

and armed with cruel hate,
On earth is not his equal.
Did we in our own strength confide,
our striving would be losing,
Were not the right Man on our side,
the man of God's own choosing;
Dost ask who that may be? Christ Jesus
it is He; Lord Sabaoth His name,
From age to age the same,
And He must win the battle.
And though this world with devils
filled should threaten to undo us,
We will not fear for God has willed
his truth to triumph through us.
The Prince of Darkness grim,
We tremble not for him;
His rage we can endure, for lo, his doom is sure;
One little word shall fell him.
That word above all earthly powers,
no thanks to them, abideth;
The Spirit and the truth are ours through
him who with us sideth; Let goods and
kindred go, this mortal life also;
The body they may kill: God's
truth abideth still;
His kingdom is forever. Amen!

Martin Luther, A Mighty Fortress Is Our God

God is our refuge and strength,
a very present help in trouble.
Therefore we will not fear though
the earth should change,

though the mountains shake in the heart of the sea;
though its waters roar and foam,
though the mountains tremble with its tumult.
There is a river whose streams make glad the city of God,
the holy habitation of the Most High.
God is in the midst of her, she shall not be moved;

God will help her right early.
The nations rage, the kingdoms totter;
he utters his voice, the earth melts.
The Lord of hosts is with us;
the God of Jacob is our refuge.
Come, behold the works of the Lord,
how he has wrought desolation in the earth.

He makes wars cease to the end of the earth;
he breaks the bow, and shatters the spear,
he burns the chariots with fire!
"Be still and know that I am God.
I am exalted among the nations,
I am exalted in the earth."
The Lord of hosts is with us;
the God of Jacob is our refuge.

Psalm 46

For thus said the Lord God,
the Holy One of Israel,
"In returning and rest you shall be saved;
In quietness and in trust shall
be your strength."

Isaiah 30:15

Do you sometimes panic when your world changes rapidly? Could you learn to be still and trust God in such situations? What difference would it make to be unfreakable – to feel secure in God as your mighty fortress, your refuge and strength?

day 32

UNFREAKABILITY: THE ART OF QUIETING THE MIND

In a world of noise pollution and hyperactivity, the great text from Psalm 46 is tough to obey: "Be still and know that I am God." Be still, let it be, let go, relax—all could be used as translations of the Hebrew. Unfortunately, the translation of words does not easily translate into experience.

American singer Bobby McFerrin made a fortune out of a very simple ditty, "Don't worry! Be happy!" There was not much new and profound about the song but it reached a lot of people in a profound way.

"Be still!" That ancient truth is being emphasized more and more in this so-called Age of Aquarius. Meditation is recommended by ancient and New Age religions to focus and center our lives. The question remains: Around what will we center our lives? In the answer to that question lies the secret to unfreakability.

At one point, Martin Luther was a man who stood against the world. Surrounded by the princes of the earth and the powers of the church, Luther kept his head, literally and figuratively. "Unless I am shown out of the Bible, I neither can nor will take back anything. My conscience is a captive to the Bible, and I cannot go against conscience. God help me. Amen."

Luther gained strength from Psalm 46. It was the passage on which he based his great hymn of the Reformation, "A Mighty Fortress Is Our God." Luther knew WHO was at the center of his life. He knew wherein his own strength lay. After striving for so many years to find peace with God, Luther found it by being still before God, even as he read, "The just shall live by faith."

All of us lose our heads from time to time. It is difficult not to freak out occasionally in this rapidly changing and highly turbulent world. We start to worry about everything as though we could do something about it. Most times we cannot. The best we can do is try to remain calm and use our energies wisely. Without centering on God that is not likely to happen.

One of my favorite stories tells of a man walking down a path one day only to see a bird nearby, lying with its feet up in the air. The man, thinking the bird was dead, started to pick it up and clear the path, when he suddenly realized the bird was alive. He said to the bird, "What are you doing?" The bird said, "I am holding up the sky." The man said, "Don't be silly. A small bird like you is not strong enough to hold up the sky." The bird replied, "One does what one can!"

We would all freak out less if we had the attitude of the bird. With the help of God, one does what one can. None of us is going to save the world, save ourselves, or save our children. Only God can do that. Meanwhile we do what we can with God's help.

"If you can keep your head when all those about you are losing theirs, then you just don't understand." So goes the current parody of Rudyard Kipling's poem, "If–." Thank God people who do understand are able to keep their heads by being still before God. If we have had our "still moments," we will be unfreakable—not always, no one is that good, but quiet times bring quiet minds when the crisis strikes. We may not hold up the sky but we will do what we can. "Be still and know that I am God."

giving and receiving **day 33**

In giving lies a power
that makes the poor cower;
They are recipients of grace
without any face.
Without freedom of choice
they have no voice.
The rich in their largesse
exhibit little finesse.
How many who wish to be kind
ever use their mind?
They have little clarity
about the effects of charity.
Giving makes you feel better
unless you have ever been debtor.
Receiving seldom helps givers grow
for it is usually "quid pro quo."
But if you cannot give in return,
your dignity becomes a concern.
The Bible says, "It is in giving
that we discover abundant living."
But if the giver does not understand receiving,
his giving can be very deceiving.
Giving relieves a sense of guilt
when self-indulgence is going full-tilt.
It gives a subtle sense of pride
behind which it is too easy to hide.
Giving demands that we take great care—
"the gift without the giver is bare."

Samuel Johnson Lindamood

If there is among you a poor man, one of your brethren, in any of your towns within your land which the Lord your God gives you, you shall not harden your heart or shut your hand against your poor brother, but you shall open your hand to him, and lend him sufficient for his need, whatever it may be.

Deuteronomy 15:7-8

And he sat down opposite the treasury, and watched the multitude putting money into the treasury. Many rich people put in large sums. And a poor widow came, and put in two copper coins, which make a penny. And he called his disciples to him, and said to them, "Truly, I say to you, this poor widow has put in more than all those who are contributing to the treasury. For they all contributed out of their abundance; but she out of her poverty has put in everything she had, her whole living.

Mark 12:41-44

Consider the lilies, how they grow; they neither toil nor spin; yet I tell you, even Solomon in all his glory was not arrayed like one of these. But if God so clothes the grass which is alive in the field today and tomorrow is thrown into the oven, how much more will he clothe you, O men of little faith! And do not seek what you are to eat and what you are to drink, nor be of anxious mind. For all the nations of the world seek these things; and your Father knows that you need them. Instead, seek his kingdom, and these things shall be yours as well.

Fear not, little flock, for it is your Father's good pleasure to give you the kingdom. Sell your possessions, and give alms; provide yourselves with purses that do not grow old, with a treasure in the heavens that does not fail, where no thief approaches and no moth destroys. For where your treasure is, there will your heart be also.

Luke 12:27-34

My brethren, show no partiality as you hold the faith of our Lord Jesus Christ, the Lord of glory. For if a man with gold rings and in fine clothing comes into your assembly, and a poor man in shabby clothing also comes in, and you pay attention to the one who wears the fine clothing and say, "Have a seat here, please," while you say to the poor man, "stand there," or "Sit at my feet," have you not made distinctions among yourselves, and become judges with evil thoughts? Listen, my beloved brethren, has not God chosen those who are poor in the world to be rich in faith and heirs of

day 33

the kingdom he has promised to those who love him? But you have dishonored the poor man. Is it not the rich who oppress you, is it not they who drag you into court? Is it not they who blaspheme that honorable name by which you are called?...

What does it profit, my brethren, if a man says he has faith but has not works? Can his faith save him? If a brother or sister is ill-clad and in lack of daily food, and one of you says to them, "Go in peace, be warmed and filled," without giving them the things needed for the body, what does it profit? So faith by itself, if it has no works, is dead.

James 2:1-6, 14-17

In all things I have shown you that by so toiling one must help the weak, remembering the words of the Lord Jesus, how he said, 'It is more blessed to give than to receive.'

Acts 20:35

day 33

GIVING AND RECIEVING

A good part of my life has been spent among people of means; professionally, I have worked with people who have great wealth. The number of gracious givers is few.

Most giving is conditional; there are strings attached. "Respond as I wish you to and there will be more where that gift came from." Such reasoning often underlies our giving and makes it terribly manipulative. Tragic but true!

It is even more difficult to be a good receiver. Most people do not wish "to be in debt to anyone." Correspondingly, they are unable to receive well because, almost before they can express gratitude, they are looking for ways to repay, quickly.

Our society is based on a "quid pro quo" philosophy—this for that, tit for tat, ying for yang, gift for gift. You send me a Christmas card, I send you a Christmas card. You give me a party, I give you a party. You send my child a graduation gift, I send your child a graduation gift.

Some people keep an extra present around the house at Christmas just in case someone drops by with a present unexpectedly. Quickly, then, they can wrap the gift and repay the debt. There is little joy in such receiving!

One of the burdens of growing older gracefully is the problem of receiving. As our eyesight dims and our strength diminishes, we are often less able to help others. Our debt to those who help us grows. If we live a long time, we grow more and more in debt unless we change our attitude about receiving. An older woman hates to lose her driver's license because it makes her more dependent and more in debt. Learning to be an independent dependent is impossible without learning to receive well.

Our response to God is often as confused. Grace is unacceptable because it is freely given. We can't repay God and that makes us very uneasy; there must be some catch. We mostly operate on a premise of "getting what you deserve." We think we get what we deserve because we are such good people and deserve what we get. It makes sense for God to love us. None of this free grace for us; we would rather not be in debt to God.

Faith should teach us the lesson of receiving from a gracious God who does not condition love. God's love, agape, is "unconquerable benevolence, invincible good will," always reaching out to redeem. "God so loved the world that He gave..."

To receive God's love is to recognize who God is and who we are. That can be scary. To receive in such a way that gratitude and love are conveyed to the giver is, perhaps, the greatest gift we can give another. What seems the height of irony, even a contradictory idea, turns out to be one of the great secrets of life—through receiving graciously, we give in return. Amen!

growing old gracefully day 34

A group of writers composed largely of men with whom I meet regularly gave me an insight into this view of life. When I told them about this book, they became somewhat sad, as if I were entering a delicate, almost ghostly realm, where there was much that might not be spoken of. Death and old age felt synonymous to them. One suggested I ask each woman to talk to me about her mother's death as a way of edging up on the subject of her own. It struck me that these men saw life in a linear fashion and that old age for them was the end of a line leading straight to the grave.

This was not the response I found among the women themselves; to them the grave does not loom straight ahead. Rather they spoke about living as part of a cyclic process and of death as part of that cycle of life. There was a feeling of a spiral toward knowledge and of wholeness, completion, the way a circle is complete. There was anxiety about the prospect of ill health and frailty. A universal dread is the nursing home, but I found very little fear of death. Rather there was a strong desire to live as long as health and functioning last. These women expressed an enormous *joie de vivre*, interest, excitement, adventurousness, passion.

At eighty-two the analyst Florida Scott-Maxwell wrote in her journal that she felt more passionate in her later years than ever before. Her diary offers insight, too, into the nature of a woman's attitude toward death. She wrote that in her old age she believed her psyche had become complete, and yet there were times she felt she was scarcely here at all. She remembered pregnancies: in the last months the child seemed to claim almost all of her body, leaving her uncertain as to whether her life was her own. She asked, "Is life a pregnancy? That would make death a birth." Perhaps biology determines our attitudes throughout the whole of life.

Charlotte Painter, Gifts Of Age

Cowards die many times before their deaths;
The valiant never taste of death but once.
Of all the wonders that I yet have heard,
It seems to me most strange
that men should fear;
Seeing that death, a necessary end,
Will come when it will come

Shakespeare, Julius Caesar

Each man goes home before he dies. Each man, as I, physically or mentally, it does not matter which, goes shivering up the dark stairs, carrying a taper that set gigantic shadows reeling in his brain. He pushes through the cobwebs of unopened doors. Or, rich and happy in his memories, he runs swiftly up the steps of a mansion that has no terrors and bursts into the lighted room of peace to find the fire dead upon the grate and the rocking chair still swaying slightly. "Wait, wait," he desperately entreats, but the last spark goes out upon the hearth and a rising wind slams the door behind him in a fury of postponed violence.

Loren Eiseley, All The Strange Hours

Sometimes I feel my age
For, truly I am old.
Well past the Bible's three score years and ten.
Now aches and pains,
And creaking joints,
And failing sight,
Are fully felt,
(Though not admitted.)
'Tis then the sadness of the
World o'erwhelms me.
AND THEN—there are days
When this ancient body
Pulses with life,
When the day ahead is bright with promise
And joy!
Speaks of love and loved ones
And friends who care.
'Tis then the gladness of the world delights me.

day 34

> I thank you, Lord, for these days.
> And the others?
> Well they are YOUR days, too, Lord.
>
> *Ruth Greig (age 94)*

Remember your creator in the days of your youth, before the days of trouble come, and the years draw near when you will say, "I have no pleasure in them"; before the sun and the light and the moon and the stars are darkened and the clouds return with the rain; in the day when the guards of the house tremble, and the strong men are bent, and the women who grind cease working because they are few, and those who look through the windows see dimly; when the doors on the street are shut, and the sound of the grinding is low, and one rises up at the sound of a bird, and all the daughters of song are brought low; when one is afraid of heights, and terrors are in the road; the almond tree blossoms, the grasshopper drags itself along and desire fails; because all must go to their eternal home, and the mourners will go about the streets; before the silver cord is snapped, and the golden bowl is broken, and the pitcher is broken at the fountain, and the wheel broken at the cistern, and the dust returns to the earth as it was, and the breath returns to God who gave it. Vanity of vanities, says the Teacher; all is vanity.

Ecclesiastes 12:1-8 (NRSV)

GROWING OLD GRACEFULLY

Recently I had a significant birthday (some say they are all significant) and it gave me pause. It was an occasion of joy, tinged by sorrow. My daughters gave me a scrapbook made up of letters and pictures and anecdotes from long-time friends. I was very pleased when I read it and occasionally a bit melancholic.

I realized once again that my life was passing before me; so many wonderful friends who wrote such good things to me had had such bad things happen to them. The accidental death of children, the suicide of a spouse, the aches and pains that come with old age, the ravages of serious illness, the fragile nature of human life—it was all there before my eyes. I rejoiced and was sad at the same time.

Now as I face retirement and see what has happened to so many friends, the problem of growing old gracefully is very real. Professionally I have been working with older friends and parishioners for years. But now it is different, existential I believe we call it. Retirement here I come.

Perhaps it is good to be growing older at a time when our society is growing in the number of older people. Examples abound of what it means to grow old gracefully. Unfortunately, examples also abound of how not to grow old gracefully.

It obviously has little to do with the problems that life presents us. Visit two people with the same problems, widows with crippling arthritis for example, or two older people neither of whom can hear well or see well, very dependent. One will be cheerful and full of life; the other will be complaining and unpleasant. Their problems superficially are the same, their attitudes amazingly different.

What makes the difference? We are still only making calculated guesses. The chances are that the attitudes of old age are merely exaggerations of the attitudes with which we have lived our lives. If we have been picky and hard to live with as young people, we are not likely to change when we are old. If we have lived with some sense of joy and gratitude for what God has given us, that response is not likely to change either.

Serenity and graciousness are attitudes enhanced by faith, even if that faith is slightly unorthodox. One of the loveliest older women I have known was very calm in facing death and the process of dying, yet she did not believe in the resurrection. Whereas I might say that God gifted her with that serenity, she would not lay claim to the Giver. Her faith, unorthodox as it was, was a major factor in the graceful way she lived her last days.

Having a sense of humor and a sense of God will give anyone a livelier outlook on life. What's inside of us is much more important than what's outside of us. As we get older we can take a vacation from many of the problems that beset us, but we can never take a vacation from ourselves. The sad truth remains: we are too soon old, too late smart.

One definition of graceful means "the quality of being attractive." Older people who keep their sense of vitality and joy for living are immensely attractive, no matter what their appearance. They are "growing old gracefully."

God grant us all that gift!

the compassionate beast day 35

There's so much good in the worst of us,
And so much bad in the best of us,
That it doesn't behoove any of us
To talk about the rest of us.

Anonymous

Thus the stubbornness and depth of man's idolatry makes any basic self-improvement in him virtually impossible. "For the mind that is set on the flesh is hostile to God; it does not submit to God's law, indeed it cannot." (Romans 8:7) And even though man's inability to change himself radically for the better is a central tenet of the Christian belief, it would often seem "There needs no ghost, my lord, come from the grave to tell us this" (Hamlet). Observation and reason tell us this. Albert Einstein, a personification of reason in our time, could observe: "Things always remain essentially the same. Nations continue to fall into the same trap, because atavistic drives are more powerful than reason or acquired convictions." On another occasion the famous scientist could say: "The real problem is in the hearts of men...It is easier to change the nature of plutonium than man's evil spirit." The church fully agrees. Faith in God through Christ and faith in human nature are two totally different faiths. This is why Herbert Butterfield can tell us that "it is essential not to have faith in human nature." Such faith is a recent heresy and a very disastrous one.

Robert L. Short, The Parables Of Peanuts

When I say that all men have a mind which cannot bear to see the sufferings of others, my meaning may be illustrated thus: even now-a-days, if men suddenly see a child about to fall into a well, they will without exception experience a feeling of alarm and distress. They will feel so, not as a ground on which they may gain the favour of the child's parents, nor as a ground on which they may seek the praise of their neighbours and friends, nor from a dislike to the reputation of having been unmoved by such a thing.

From this case we may perceive that the feeling of commiseration is essential to man, that the feeling of shame and dislike is essential to man, that the feeling of modesty and complaisance is essential to man, and that the feeling of approving and disapproving is essential to man.

The feeling of commiseration is the principle of benevolence. The feeling of shame and dislike is the principle of righteousness. The feeling of modesty and complaisance is the principle of propriety. The feeling of approving and disapproving is the principle of knowledge.

Mencius, James Legge translation

None is righteous, no, not one;
no one understands, no one seeks for God.
All have turned aside, together
they have gone wrong;
no one does good, not even one.
Their throat is an open grave,
they use their tongues to deceive.
The venom of asps is under their lips.
Their mouth is full of curses and bitterness.
Their feet are swift to shed blood,
in their paths are ruin and misery,
and the way of peace they do not know.
Their is no fear of God before their eyes.

Romans 3:10-18

Can the Ethiopian change his skin or the leopard his spots? Then also you can do good who are accustomed to do evil.

Jeremiah 13:23

Unless one is born anew, he cannot see the kingdom of God." Nicodemus said to him, "How can a man be born when he is old? Can he enter a second time into his mother's womb and be born?"

John 3:3-4

day 35

What do you think: are human beings basically good or basically evil? Is it still necessary for a "good" person to be saved? Why or why not?

day 35

THE COMPASSIONATE BEAST

Have you heard of "altruism research"? I have been immersed in two books on the subject. It may be a new subject for research, but it's an ancient debate. What is the nature of the beast? Are human beings basically good, bad, or neutral? Are we closer to the animals or the angels?

The Bible seems to waste little time debating the issue. Human nature, from the time of Adam, has been fallen, corrupted, sinful, and in need of redemption. American cartoonist William Steig famously and bluntly put it this way: "People are no damn good."

Orthodox Christianity from its inception has assumed the evil nature of humankind. There was a brief flirtation with Pelagius who didn't think humans were all that bad, but Saint Augustine stood for the orthodox and won the day. Down through the centuries that position has been maintained.

Certain doctrines are changing, however, such as ideas about the baptism of infants. We used to affirm "the damnation of infants." Baptism was a rite of cleansing for their "dirty little souls." We didn't say it that way, but that's what we meant. That's changing! Our congregation today wants to celebrate the new life of a child, to rejoice with the parents in God's gift. They do not wish to celebrate the child's "rightness" with God through the sprinkling of water. The child is okay in the eyes of God already. They know the child is not perfect, but they certainly don't view the child as being abhorrently bad.

Altruism research raises some interesting questions for us. How do we explain the desire to do good from those who are not redeemed from their sins, or at least don't claim to be? Is there an altruistic gene or complex of genes? If not, is it likely that the proclivity and capacity for altruism are born in us?

My years as a pastor leave me with mixed feelings. The "happy pagan" friends with whom I grew up were as altruistic as my so-called "redeemed friends." Over and over again I have held memorial services for people whom their friends assured me were "good folk" though not practicing Christians.

Having a proclivity or capacity for altruism, however, is not enough. The effect of sin is very real in all our lives. More often than not, sin will overcome our altruism. We still need to be changed. Jeremiah's question is more germane: "Can the Ethiopian change his skin or the leopard his spots?" Can we bring about a change in human nature that will enlarge upon any altruistic genes or proclivities for good?

Changing human nature is difficult at best, but we are offered that glorious possibility. "If a person is in Christ, he or she is a new creation. The old has passed away, behold, the new has come." Our proclivities and capacities, our good and our bad, are included in that great hope.

Altruism research has given us data on a more compassionate beast, but God has given us hope that we can be even better. We are not angel, nor animal, nor angelic-animal, but fully human and trying to realize our potential with the help of God.

the will of god day 36

What God's will is and how to find it was inadequate for the kinds of decisions I was having to make in my own life. I had been taught that God's will was something objective, out there, that I could go and find, that would come clear to me. And as I looked for it and looked for it and looked for it, I began to feel more and more that it was a needle somewhere in that haystack, and I didn't have a prayer of finding it. And yet if I didn't find it, I would make some awful mistake, and how terrible that would be.

I don't believe that anymore. Providence for me is meaningful in retrospect but not in prospect. I think now that God has set us free to be responsible to make our own choices and to pay the costs for them, with our eyes wide open and our feet on the ground, and that God goes with us, goes before us, and meets us at every corner; and that there isn't one option that he has in mind that we have to find somehow among all those options. We do the best we can. We make our decisions and choices. We make mistakes. At every turning and corner, God is there with us as the images within us break, helping us to put back the pieces, but now in a new shape and a new pattern. And with a new tenderness and a new humility because only those who are broken or have been broken or are breaking can really understand what it is that may be breaking in other people.

Robert A. Raines, Success Is A Moving Target

Our view of reality is like a map with which to negotiate the terrain of life. If the map is true and accurate, we will generally know where we are, and if we have decided where we want to go, we will generally know how to get there. If the map is false and inaccurate, we generally will be lost.

While this is obvious, it is something that most people to a greater or lesser degree choose to ignore. They ignore it because our route to reality is not easy. First of all, we are not born with maps; we have to make them, and the making requires effort. The more effort we make to appreciate and perceive reality, the larger and more accurate our maps will be. But many do not want to make this effort. Some stop making it by the end of adolescence. Their maps are small and sketchy, their views of the world narrow and misleading. By the end of middle age most people have given up the effort. They feel certain that their maps are complete and their *Weltanshauung* is correct (indeed, even sacrosanct), and they are no longer interested in new information. It is as if they are tired. Only a relative and fortunate few continue until the moment of death exploring the mystery of reality, ever enlarging and refining and redefining their understand of the world and what is true.

But the biggest problem of map-making is not that we have to start from scratch, but that if our maps are to be accurate we have to continually revise them....We are daily bombarded with new information as to the nature of reality. If we are to incorporate this information, we must continually revise our maps, and sometimes when enough new information has accumulated, we must make very major revisions. The process of making revisions, particularly major revisions, is painful, sometimes excruciatingly painful. And herein lies the major source of many of the ills of mankind...

What we do more often than not, and usually unconsciously, is to ignore the new information. Often this act of ignoring is much more than passive. We may denounce the new information as false, dangerous, heretical, the work of the devil. We may actually crusade against it, and even attempt to manipulate the world so as to make it conform to our view of reality. Rather than try to change the map, an individual may try to destroy the new reality. Sadly, such a person may expend much more energy ultimately in defending an outmoded view of the world than would have been required to revise and correct it in the first place.

Scott Peck, The Road Less Traveled

day 36

Whither, midst falling dew,
While glow the heavens with
the last steps of day,
Far through their rosy depths dost thou pursue
Thy solitary way?
Vainly the fowler's eye
Might mark thy distant flight, to do thee wrong,
As, darkly painted on the crimson sky,
Thy figure floats along.
Seek'st thou the plashy brink
Of weedy lake, or marge of river wide,
Or where the rocking billows rise and sink
On the chafed ocean-side?
There is a Power whose care
Teaches thy way along that pathless coast—
The desert and illimitable air—
Lone wandering, but not lost.
All day thy wings have fanned,
At that far height, the cold, thin atmosphere;
Yet stoop not, weary, to the welcome land,
Though the dark night is near.
And soon that toil shall end;
Soon shalt thou find a summer home, and rest,
And scream among thy fellows;
Reeds shall bend soon o'er thy sheltered nest.
Thou'rt gone; the abyss of Heaven
Hath swallowed up thy form; yet on my heart
Deeply hath sunk the lesson thou hast given,
And shall not soon depart.
He, who from zone to zone
Guides through the boundless
sky thy certain flight,
In the long way that I must tread alone,
Will lead my steps aright.

William Cullen Bryant, To A Waterfowl

Therefore, since we are justified by faith, we have peace with God through our Lord Jesus Christ. Through him we have obtained access to this grace in which we stand, and we rejoice in our hope of sharing the glory of God. More than that, we rejoice in our sufferings, knowing that suffering produces endurance, and endurance produces character, and character produces hope, and hope does not disappoint us, because God's love has been poured into our hearts through the Holy Spirit which has been given to us.

Romans 5:1-5

We know that in everything God works for good with those who love him, who are called according to his purpose. For those whom he foreknew he also predestined to be conformed to the image of his Son, in order that he might be the first-born among many brethren. And those whom he predestined he also called; and those whom he called he also justified; and those whom he justified he also glorified. What then shall we say to this? If God is for us, who is against us?

Romans 8:28-31

I appeal to you, therefore, brethren, by the mercies of God, to present your bodies as a living sacrifice, holy and acceptable to God, which is your spiritual worship. Do not be conformed to this world but be transformed by the renewal of your mind, that you may prove what is the will of God, what is good and acceptable and perfect.

Romans 12:1-2

Therefore, my beloved, as you have always obeyed, so now, not only as in my presence but much more in my absence, work out your own salvation with fear and trembling; for God is at work in you, both to will and to work for his good pleasure.

Philippians 2:12-13

Come now, you who say, "Today or tomorrow we will go into such and such a town and spend a year there and trade and get gain"; whereas you do not know about tomorrow. What is your life? For you are a mist that appears for a little time and then vanishes. Instead you ought to say, "If the Lord wills, we shall live and we shall do this or that."

James 4:13-15

day 36

THE WILL OF GOD

The two nuns stood with downcast eyes, hands folded in prayer. The priest, almost in chanting fashion, was intoning to our friend, "Naked we came into the world. Naked shall we return. The Lord gives and the Lord takes away. Blessed be the name of the Lord." My spirit rose up in protest at this merciless statement of the will of God.

My friend, an older confrere in the Presbyterian ministry, had just lost his recently acquired wife and child in a drowning accident. The horror of it was almost too much to take in and now the cold statement of scripture was repugnant. The will of God had always been unclear to me, but I was very clear that those deaths were not the will of God as I saw it.

Now, over thirty years later, my mind has not changed. In fact, the will of God becomes more an open possibility all the time. Much like going to an Automobile Association to get advice on various possible routes to take on a driving vacation, so the will of God may lead us down numerous avenues.

Agnosticism, for me, often seems the better way when talking about the will of God. It certainly is easier to make better judgments about God's will in retrospect than it is in prospect, but even that I find slightly suspect. Logic says we shouldn't think we can know God's will since we aren't God, but logic has little to do with certain aspects of Christian theology.

Presumption abounds!

I, for one, agree with the wag who said, "I would rather see coming toward me a regiment with drawn sword than one lone Calvinist convinced he was doing the will of God." Amen.

If the will of God is closed, set in concrete so to speak, we are all in deep trouble. It does not appear that any amount of thought, meditation, prayer, worship, or any other means is going to reveal God's will for each of us.

If, on the other hand, the will of God for us is open to many possibilities, then it brings to our life an excitement. Life is full of opportunities to try and serve God wherever we can, however we can. To face the world in which we live today with openness is a greater challenge that requires far more courage, far more faith that God is with us, than to believe in some closed system where things are set and can only be done one way.

English Christian theologian Leslie Weatherhead once drew a distinction between the intentional will of God, the circumstantial will of God, and the ultimate will of God. It strikes me as just too neat, too pat. It is a helpful framework within which to discuss the will of God but not much better than any other when it comes to knowing the will of God.

St. Paul's statement to the Philippians seems so clearly open-ended: "Therefore, my beloved, as you have always obeyed, so now, not only as in my presence but much more in my absence, work out your own salvation with fear and trembling; for God is at work in you, both to will and to work for his good pleasure" (Phil. 2:12-13).

I prefer such "fear and trembling" to a pious certainty which claims to be faith.

the wonder of grace day 37

Amazing grace! How sweet the sound
That saved a wretch like me!
I once was lost, but now am found,
Was blind, but now I see.
'Twas grace that taught my heart to fear,
And grace my fears relieved;
How precious did that grace appear
The hour I first believed.
Through many dangers, toils and snares,
I have already come;
'Tis grace hath brought me safe thus far,
And grace will lead me home.

John Newton, Amazing Grace

The Lord said to Moses, "Say to Aaron and his sons, Thus you shall bless the people of Israel: you shall say to them,
The Lord bless you and keep you:
The Lord make his face to shine upon you, and be gracious to you:
The Lord lift up his countenance upon you, and give you peace.
"So shall they put my name upon the people of Israel, and I will bless them."

Numbers 6:22-27

For God so loved the world that he gave his only son, that whoever believes in him should not perish but have eternal life. For God sent the Son into the world, not to condemn the world, but that the world might be saved through him.

John 3:16-18

While we were yet helpless, at the right time Christ died for the ungodly. Why, one will hardly die for a righteous man--though perhaps for a good man one will dare even to die. But God shows his loves for us in that while we were yet sinners, Christ died for us.

Romans 5:6-8

But by the grace of God I am what I am, and his grace toward me was not in vain. On the contrary, I worked harder than any of them, though it was not I, but the grace of God which is with me.

I Corinthians 15:10

For the grace of God has appeared for the salvation of all men, training us to renounce irreligion and worldly passions, and to live sober, upright, and godly lives in this world, awaiting our blessed hope, the appearing of the glory of our great God and Savior Jesus Christ, who gave himself for us to redeem us from all iniquity and to purify for himself a people of his own who are zealous for good deeds.

Titus 2:11-14

Grace be to you, and peace, from God our Father and the Lord Jesus Christ.

Ephesians 1:2

But God, who is rich in mercy, out of the great love with which he loved us, even when we were dead through our trespasses, made us alive together with Christ (by grace you have been saved), and raised us up with him, and made us sit with him in the heavenly places in Christ Jesus, that in the coming ages he might show the immeasurable riches of his grace in kindness toward us in Christ Jesus. For by grace you have been saved through faith; and this is not your own doing, it is the gift of God—not because of works, lest any man should boast. For we are his workmanship, created in Christ Jesus for good works, which God prepared beforehand, that we should walk in them.

Ephesians 2:4-10

day 37

Have you ever experienced a moment of grace when you felt sure you were loved and accepted by God? If so, what difference did it make in your life? If not, what do you imagine such an experience would mean to you?

day 37

THE WONDER OF GRACE

One time long ago I was sick and lying in bed, reading an inspirational book about the Christian ministry. I do not remember anything extraordinary happening except that I was overwhelmed by the feeling that God loved ME and that God was present with me. I felt at the moment as though I could have committed my life to any "call," even risk death, and it would all be all right. God would give me the strength. That was a powerful moment in the life of a young man, a moment of grace.

Despite the years that have passed, I still remember the moment well; the accompanying feeling is now not as strong. Thirty-five years in the ministry with their besetting problems have dimmed the strength of that early experience, but they have dimmed neither the wonder of grace nor my love for the wonder-full world of grace in which we live.

"You are accepted!" Such an experience of grace is almost too good to be true. The State of California once had a Commission on Self-Esteem—the California Task Force to Promote Self-Esteem and Personal and Social Responsibility, famously lampooned by cartoonist Gary Trudeau in a 1986 New York Times column—but, unfortunately, it knew very little about God or grace. We are too much into "pumping ourselves up" and not enough into "letting grace strike." Getting "into yourself," as the recommendation seems to be these days, often produces the opposite of what's hoped for. Focusing on one's self has never brought greater self-acceptance and self-esteem.

Some Christians, on the other hand, would tell us that there is a formula by which you can experience grace. "If you confess with your mouth the Lord Jesus, you shall be saved."

Would that such a simple verbal expression would truly bring people the "feeling of grace." Being accepted and feeling accepted are not necessarily one and the same thing.

The mystery remains that God would love us at all and no recitation of formulas is likely to overcome that mystery. For those who think grace can be found through "four spiritual laws," more power to them. For me, the image of "being struck" is greater.

"Being struck" means that we don't have as much control over the experience of grace. "Amazing grace" is amazing because we are not able to control it. It is God's gift, and we can only receive and respond. "You are accepted!" Wonder-full!

The frightening and wonderful part about grace is that we experience it most in human relationships. We are able both to receive and to give love in such ways that our relationships may produce the experience of grace. I say "may" because grace cannot be forced. Grace is a gift, from God or another human being.

Grace transforms the world into a wonder-full place because we are so in awe of it. How can such love be? Is it really true? What a difference it makes! Life continues as is, but everything is different. "What a difference a day makes" when you have been struck by grace. English clergyman John Newton knew the experience:

"Amazing grace! How sweet the sound

That saved a wretch like me!

I once was lost, but now am found,

Was blind, but now I see."

security in every season day 38

And if you obey the voice of the Lord your God, being careful to do all his commandments which I command you this day, the Lord your God will set you high above all the nations of the earth. And all these blessings shall come upon you and overtake you, if you obey the voice of the Lord your God. Blessed shall you be in the city, and blessed shall you be in the field. Blessed shall be the fruit of your body, and the fruit of your ground, and the fruit of your beasts, the increase of your cattle, and the young of your flock. Blessed shall be your basket and your kneading-trough. Blessed shall you be when you come in, and blessed shall you be when you go out.

Deuteronomy 28:1-6

He who dwells in the shelter of the Most High,
who abides in the shadow of the Almighty,
will say to the Lord, "My refuge and my fortress;
my God, in whom I trust."
For he will deliver you from
the snare of the fowler
and from the deadly pestilence;
he will cover you with his pinions,
and under his wings you will find refuge;
his faithfulness is a shield and buckler.
You will not fear the terror of the night,
nor the arrow that flies by day,
nor the pestilence that stalks in darkness,
nor the destruction that wastes at noonday.
A thousand may fall at your side,
ten thousand at your right hand;
but it will not come near you.
You will only look with your eyes
and see the recompense of the wicked.
Because you have made the Lord your refuge,
the Most High your habitation,
no evil shall befall you,
no scourge come near your tent.
For he will give his angels charge of you
to guard you in all your ways.
On their hands they will bear you up,
lest you dash your foot against a stone.
You will tread on the lion and the adder,
the young lion and the serpent
you will trample under foot.
Because he cleaves to me in love,
I will deliver him.
I will protect him, because he knows my name.
When he calls to me, I will answer him;
I will be with him in trouble,
I will rescue him and honor him.
With long life I will satisfy him
and show him my salvation.

Psalm 91

Unless the Lord builds the house,
those who build it labor in vain.
Unless the Lord watches over the city,
the watchman stays awake in vain.
It is in vain that you rise up early and go late to rest,
eating the bread of anxious toil;
for he gives to his beloved sleep.

Psalm 127:1-2

I waited patiently for the Lord;
he inclined to me and heard my cry.
He drew me up from the desolate pit,
out of the miry bog,
and set my feet upon a rock,
making my steps secure.
He put a new song in my mouth,
a song of praise to our God.

Psalm 40:1-3

The Lord is my shepherd,
I shall not want;
He maketh me to lie down in green pastures.
He leadeth me beside the still waters;
he restoreth my soul.
He leadeth in the paths of righteousness

day 38

for his name's sake.
Yea, though I walk through the valley
of the shadow of death,
I will fear no evil;
For thou art with me;
thy rod and thy staff
they comfort me.
Thou preparest a table before me
in the presence of mine enemies.
Thou anointest my head with oil,
my cup runneth over.
Surely goodness and mercy shall follow me
all the days of my life;
And I shall dwell in the house of the Lord
forever. Amen!

Psalm 23 (KJV)

He who walks in integrity walks securely, but he who perverts his ways will be found out.

He who winks the eye causes trouble, but he who boldly reproves makes peace.

The mouth of the righteous is a fountain of life, but the mouth of the wicked conceals violence.

Hatred stirs up strife, but love covers all offenses.

Proverbs 10:9-12

Put on the whole armor of God, that you may be able to stand against the wiles of the devil. For we are not contending against flesh and blood, but against the principalities, against the powers, against the world rulers of this present darkness, against the spiritual hosts of wickedness in the heavenly places. Therefore take the whole armor of God, that you may be able to withstand in the evil day, and having done all, to stand. Stand therefore, having girded your loins with truth, and having put on the breastplate of righteousness, and having shod your feet with the equipment of the gospel of peace; besides all these, taking the shield of faith, with which you can quench all the flaming darts of the evil one. And take the helmet of salvation, and the sword of the Spirit, which is the word of God.

Ephesians 6:11-17

day 38

SECURITY IN EVERY SEASON

Over the course of my life there has been an abundance of stuffed animals—a tiger, a bunny, a bear, a Snoopy, a bunch of frogs—others which I have forgotten, but all of which I have loved. I must admit I still love the feel of a stuffed animal. Why something soft and warm and snuggly gets to me so much I am not sure. Memories of childhood? Perhaps! Security? You bet!

My fondness for stuffed animals certainly reminds me of my inner child. Being able to hang on to something that does not change and finding comfort in it is good for the child in me. It is good for the adult in me.

Once I might have wanted to deny such need, to be more manly, to show that I can stand on my own two feet, that I need no one, that I am independent. No more! Hand me the stuffed animal and I will hold it. I am not afraid any longer of that child in me.

And I am certainly not afraid to admit my need for security.

Many of the greatest psalms are magnificent in their affirmation of God being our refuge, our strength, our help in time of trouble, and none more famously than Psalm 23:

"Yea, though I walk through the valley of the shadow of death, I will fear no evil; For thou art with me; thy rod and thy staff they comfort me."

We gain immense comfort from knowing that God is by our side as we walk "through the valley of the shadow of death." We long "to dwell in the shelter of the Most High" (Psalm 91). Reading those psalms is like hugging your Teddy Bear, but you don't feel embarrassed by it.

As the years have passed, I wish I had been able to keep one of my stuffed animals from childhood so that it could have aged with me. The continuity of those years would, I believe, be made richer by that presence.

There is a quiet comfort in living with something for a long time, stuffed animal or whatever. There is an even greater comfort in living for a long time with a person, such as a beloved spouse of many years. The greatest comfort is in knowing God has lived with us and loved us all those years. So I, too, shall trust my sleep to the watcher who watches over me and my stuffed animals.

wrestling through to god day 39

I suspect we have got to ask very seriously whether we should even begin our thinking about prayer in terms of the times we "set aside", whether prayer is primarily something we do in the "spaces", in the moment of disengagement from the world. I wonder whether Christian prayer, prayer in the light of the Incarnation, is not to be defined in terms of penetration through the world of God rather than withdrawal from the world of God. For the moment of revelation is precisely so often, in my experience, the moment of meeting and unconditional engagement. How easily one finds oneself giving pious advice to a person faced with a decision to "go away and pray about it." But, if I am honest, what enlightenment I have had on decisions has almost always come not when I have gone away and stood back from them, but precisely as I have wrestled through all the most practical pros and cons, usually with other people. And this activity, undertaken by a Christian trusting and expecting that God is there, would seem to be prayer.

This can perhaps be put another way by saying that traditional spirituality has placed a premium on 'the interior life', regarding this as the spiritual core of man. But Bonhoeffer points out that the Bible knows nothing of such a premium: 'The "heart" in the biblical sense is not the inward life, but the whole man in relation to God!' And he goes on to make the telling remark that for the Bible 'man lives just as much from outwards to inwards as from inwards to outwards.' This I believe to be profoundly true for great numbers of people, probably for the majority. For them 'real life is meeting.' They are, of course, subject to the rhythm of engagement and disengagement, just as the capacity of the body to function creatively depends on the quality of its relaxation... Nevertheless, and so far as an assessment is made of our physical capacity and alertness, it is made on the evidence of our waking hours. And for such people, 'their prayer is in the practice of their trade.' The need for times of withdrawal is accepted naturally, but with no pretension that these times are particularly 'holy': nor will they necessarily be more 'religious', in the sense that they are devoted to spiritual exercises. They are basically times of standing back, of consolidation, of letting love's root grow. And these may be fertilized by many different processes of action or inaction.

John A. T Robinson, Honest To God

That our sanctification did not depend upon changing our works, but in doing that for God's sake which we commonly do for our own. That it was lamentable to see how many people mistook the means for the end, addicting themselves to certain works, which they performed very imperfectly, by reason of their human or selfish regards.

That the most excellent method he had found of going to God was that of doing our common business without any view of pleasing men, and (as far as we are capable) purely for the love of God.

That it was a great delusion to think that the times of prayer ought to differ from other times; that we are as strictly obliged to adhere to God by action in the time of action as by prayer in the season of prayer.

That his prayer was nothing else but a sense of the presence of God, his soul being at that time insensible to everything but divine love; and that when the appointed times of prayer were past, he found no difference, because he still continued with God, praising and blessing him with all his might, so that he passed his life in continual joy; yet hoped that God would give him somewhat to suffer when he should grow stronger.

That we ought not to be weary of doing little things for the love of God, who regards not the greatness of the work, but the love with which it is performed. That we should not wonder if, in the beginning, we often failed in our endeavors, but that at last we should gain a habit, which will naturally produce its acts in us, without our care, and to our exceeding great delight. (Fourth Conversation)

Brother Lawrence, The Practice Of The Presence Of God

day 39

The same night he arose and took his two wives, his two maids, and his eleven children, and crossed the ford of Jabbok. He took them and sent them across the stream, and likewise everything that he had. And Jacob was left alone; and a man wrestled with him until the breaking of the day. When the man saw that he did not prevail against Jacob, he touched the hollow of his thigh; and Jacob's thigh was put out of joint as he wrestled with him. Then he said, "Let me go, for the day is breaking." But Jacob said, "I will not let you go, unless you bless me." And he said to him, "What is your name?" And he said, "Jacob." Then he said, "Your name shall no more be called Jacob, but Israel, for you have striven with God and with men, and have prevailed." Then Jacob asked him, "Tell me, I pray, your name." But he said, "Why is it that you ask my name?" And there he blessed him. So Jacob called the name of the place Peni'el, saying, "For I have seen God face to face, and yet my life is preserved." The sun rose upon him as he passed Penu'el, limping because of his thigh. Therefore to this day the Israelites do not eat the sinew of the hip which is upon the hollow of the thigh, because he touched the hollow of Jacob's thigh on the sinew of the hip.

Genesis 32:22-32

And when you pray, you must not be like the hypocrites; for they love to stand and pray in the synagogues and at the street corners, that they may be seen by men. Truly, I say to you, they have their reward. But when you pray, go into your room and shut the door and pray to your Father who is in secret; and your Father who sees in secret will reward you. And in praying do not heap up empty phrases as the Gentiles do; for they think that they will be heard for their many words. Do not be like them, for your Father knows what you need before you ask him. Pray then like this:

Our Father who art in heaven,
Hallowed be thy name.
Thy kingdom come,
Thy will be done,
On earth as it is in heaven.
Give us this day our daily bread;
And forgive us our debts,
As we forgive our debtors;
And lead us not into temptation,
But deliver us from evil.

Matthew 6:5-13

And he came out, and went, as was his custom, to the Mount of Olives; and the disciples followed him. And when he came to the place he said to them, "Pray that you may not enter into temptation." And he withdrew from them about a stone's throw, and knelt down and prayed, "Father, if thou art willing, remove this cup from me; nevertheless not my will, but thine, be done." And there appeared to him an angel from heaven, strengthening him. And being in an agony he prayed more earnestly; and his sweat became like great drops of blood falling down upon the ground. And when he rose from prayer, he came to the disciples and found them sleeping for sorrow, and he said to them, "Why do you sleep? Rise and pray that you may not enter into temptation."

Matthew 22:39-46

Likewise the Spirit helps us in our weakness; for we do not know how to pray as we ought, but the Spirit himself intercedes for us with sighs too deep for words. And he who searches the hearts of men knows what is the mind of the Spirit, because the Spirit intercedes for the saints according to the will of God.

Romans 8:26-27

day 39

WRESTLING THROUGH TO GOD

It is a common human frailty to talk too much about things of which we know too little. Holy Scripture, for instance: we tout it, but know little about it. And for a lot of lip-service but not a lot of action, try prayer. "More things are wrought by prayer than this world dreams of." We believe it; we just don't pray, at least not in a formal way.

An old maxim states that "there are no atheists in foxholes." Few there are who would not try a prayer or two, just in case. Hospital rooms abound with people who suddenly have found a desire to pray. Hamlet's words are understandable:

"My words fly up,

my thoughts remain below,

Words without thoughts

never to heaven go."

Stuck here on earth, most of us don't take time to turn our thoughts upward unless there is some good reason. The average person who claims to believe in the power of prayer spends little time at prayer, or at least does not pray in any traditional disciplined fashion. "Going into the closet to pray" is impossible because our closets are too full and our time is too short; besides, it seems like a dumb idea.

For most of us our greatest hope is the promise in Romans that "the Spirit helps us in our weakness; for we do not know how to pray as we ought, but the Spirit himself intercedes for us with sighs too deep for words."

What a wonderful promise! If prayer has something to do with sighs, then I pray a lot. The older I get the more my life is punctuated by sighs, even by groans—mostly involuntary responses to some inadequacy or my part or to some impossible demand at the heart of life. If the Spirit can interpret my sighs and groans, I have some hope.

We wrestle a lot with the problems of life and are too often overwhelmed by them. In the moment of struggle, it would be wonderful to know that the Spirit uses our groans, interceding for us with sighs too deep for words.

Unfortunately, we have mostly learned the lesson that prayer is withdrawal and intentional and quiet, while most of us are overloaded, preoccupied, and surrounded by noise. We need to understand that prayer is also a way of wrestling through all those problems and all that commotion. We need to believe that God is present to us in our engagement with life as well as our withdrawal.

One of my favorite memories is of a little old lady who talked to herself. On first approach, she seemed a bit odd. When we became friends, I learned that she wasn't talking to herself; she was talking to God. She didn't need a closet or a quiet time; she just blurted it right out. "Thank you, Lord." "I'm so grateful, Father." "Thank you, thank you, thank you."

She was an inspiration to me and everyone around her. There was nothing pious, sanctimonious, or self-serving about her. Life had not given her great things but she had made a great thing of her life. She was a living testimony to Paul's words: "Rejoice always, pray constantly, give thanks in all circumstances."

keep on keeping on **day 40**

Therefore, since we are justified by faith, we have peace with God through our Lord Jesus Christ. Through him we have obtained access to this grace in which we stand, and we rejoice in our hope of sharing the glory of God. More than that, we rejoice in our sufferings, knowing that suffering produces endurance, and endurance produces character, and character produces hope, and hope does not disappoint us, because God's love has been poured into our hearts through the Holy Spirit which has been given to us.

Romans 5:1-5

But we have this treasure in earthen vessels, to show that the transcendent power belongs to God and not to us. We are afflicted in every way, but not crushed; perplexed, but not driven to despair; persecuted but not forsaken; struck down, but not destroyed; always carrying in the body the death of Jesus, so that the life of Jesus may also be manifest in our bodies. For while we live we are always being given up to death for Jesus' sake, so that the life of Jesus may be manifested in our mortal flesh. So death is at work in us, but life in you.

...So we do not lose heart. Though our outer nature is wasting away, our inner nature is being renewed every day. For this slight momentary affliction is preparing for us an eternal weight of glory beyond all comparison, because we look not to the things that are seen but to the things that are unseen; for the things that are seen are transient, but the things that are unseen are eternal.

II Corinthians 4:7-12, 16-18

Do not be deceived; God is not mocked, for whatever a man sows, that he will also reap. For he who sows to his own flesh will from the flesh reap corruption; but he who sows to the Spirit will from the Spirit reap eternal life. And let us not grow weary in well-doing, for in due season we shall reap, if we do not lose heart.

Galatians 6:7-9

Count it all joy, my brethren, when you meet various trials, for you know that the testing of your faith produces steadfastness. And let steadfastness have its full effect, that you may be perfect and complete, lacking in nothing. . . . Blessed is the man who endures trial, for when he has stood the test he will receive the crown of life which God has promised to those who love him.

James 1:2-4, 12

Therefore, since we are surrounded by so great a cloud of witnesses, let us also lay aside every weight, and sin which clings so closely, and let us run with perseverance the race that is set before us, looking to Jesus the pioneer and perfecter of our faith, who for the joy that was set before him endured the cross, despising the shame, and is seated at the right hand of the throne of God

Consider him who endured from sinners such hostility against himself, so that you may not grow weary or fainthearted. In your struggle against sin you have not yet resisted to the point of shedding your blood. And have you forgotten the exhortation which addresses you as sons?—

"My son, do not regard lightly the discipline of the Lord,
nor lose courage when you are punished by him.
For the Lord disciplines him whom he loves,
and chastises every son whom he receives."

It is for discipline that you have to endure. God is treating you as sons; for what son is there whom his father does not discipline?

Hebrews 12:1-7

day 40

Do you ever feel that the suffering and evil in this world are too extensive and too profound for you to make a meaningful difference? What helps you to "keep on keeping on"—to continue doing the good that is in your power to do—when you're feeling compassion fatigue?

day 40

ON KEEPING ON KEEPING ON

Fatigue is a common human condition. The demands of the world are too many, but we hasten to do our best and end up dead tired. Successful men and women record hours at the office that would tire the finest athlete. Women will often "shop till they drop." Being tired is a part of our everyday experience.

Mental fatigue and compassion fatigue are much more serious; they bring an attitude of defeat and despair. "The world is no damn good." Who cares? In today's world with its monumental problems which seem to have no solution, giving up is easy.

Loren Eiseley's essay "The Star Thrower" tells the lovely story of a man who, despite seeming futility, kept throwing washed-up starfish back into the ocean with the hope that they might live. It is a parable for us. We have to keep at it, mostly in small steady ways, leaving the results to God.

This was a recurring theme in Saint Paul's letters. "So we do not lose heart. Though our outer nature is wasting away, our inner nature is being renewed every day" (II Corinthians). "And let us not grow weary in well-doing, for in due season we shall reap, if we do not lose heart" (Galatians).

Keeping those scriptures before us at the end of a frustrating day when nothing seemed to go right and no one seemed to care is difficult, but it is our only hope. Compassion fatigue is a recently invented term, but the reality is as old as life. It is hard to keep on keeping on, especially when those you are trying to help don't seem to want your help. If they don't want to help themselves, why should I waste my energy?

Good question. Answer: Because God wants us to keep on. Earthen vessels we are—some say "cracked pots"—but God uses us to better the world and we need to keep on.

Part of our problem, of course, is that we look for and expect certain results. Chances are that if it is a group project, there are goals and expectations laid out ahead of time. Goals are wonderful for planning and for focusing the use of energy, but they are destructive when it comes to measuring results. Goal-orientation produces compassion fatigue faster than almost anything because our expectations usually far exceed the possibilities.

What a joy it would be if we could just keep on keeping on and leave the results to God. "Paul planted, Apollo watered, but God gave the growth." That's hard for us to accept. Our efforts should produce tangible results and when they don't, we are tired. Dog-tired, bone-tired, weary and weighted down; give me a drink.

Quoting scripture does not solve hard problems, but those ancient truths help: "Therefore, having this ministry by the mercy of God, we do not lose heart...We are afflicted in every way, but not crushed; perplexed, but not driven to despair; persecuted, but not forsaken; struck down, but not destroyed."

The worst part for most of us is wanting to do what is right and not being able to see it happen. It ought to work this way. Why won't people listen? It's so frustrating! All of which comes from our desire to control the results.

Keeping on keeping on is possible only in faith that God will bring about the results, not ourselves. Trusting in the power of God and not in our own power will give new strength and help us to overcome debilitating compassion fatigue.

the process of taming day 41

He that is thy friend indeed,
He will help thee in thy need:
If thou sorrow, he will weep;
If thou wake, he cannot sleep:
Thus of every grief in heart
He with thee doth bear a part.
These are certain signs to know
Faithful friend from flattering foe.

Richard Barnfield, An Ode

There are men too gentle to live among wolves
Who toss them like a lost and wounded dove.
Such gentle men are lonely in a merchant's world,
Unless they have a gentle one to love.

James Kavanaugh, There Are Men Too Gentle To Live Among Wolves

The next day again John was standing with two of his disciples; and he looked at Jesus as he walked, and said, "Behold, the Lamb of God!" The two disciples heard him say this, and they turned and followed Jesus. Jesus turned, and saw them following, and said to them, "What do you seek?" And they said to him "Rabbi" (which means Teacher), "where are you staying?" He said to them, "Come and see." They came and saw where he was staying; and they stayed with him that day, for it was about the tenth hour. One of the two who heard John speak, and followed him, was Andrew, Simon Peter's brother... He first found his brother Simon, and said to him, "We have found the Messiah" (which means Christ). He brought him to Jesus. Jesus looked at him, and said, "So you are Simon the son of John? You shall be called Cephas," (which means Peter).

The next day Jesus decided to go to Galilee. And he found Philip and said to him, "Follow me." Now Philip was from Bethsaida, the city of Andrew and Peter. Philip found Nathanael, and said to him, "We have found him of whom Moses in the law and also the prophets wrote, Jesus of Nazareth, the son of Joseph."

Nathanael said to him, "Can anything good come out of Nazareth?"

Phillip said to him, "Come and see." Jesus saw Nathanael coming to him, and said of him, "Behold, an Israelite indeed, in whom there is no guile!" Nathanael said to him, "How do you know me?" Jesus answered him, "Before Philip called you, when you were under the fig tree, I saw you." Nathanael answered him, "Rabbi, you are the Son of God! You are the King of Israel!" Jesus answered him, "Because I said to you, I saw you under the fig tree, do you believe? You shall see greater things than these." And he said to him, "Truly, truly, I say to you, you will see heaven opened, and the angels of God ascending and descending upon the Son of man."

John 1:35-51

"If you abide in me, and my words abide in you, ask whatever you will, and it shall be done for you. By this my Father is glorified, that you bear much fruit, and so prove to be my disciples. As the Father has loved me, so have I loved you; abide in my love. If you keep my commandments, you will abide in my love, just as I have kept my Father's commandments and abide in his love. These things I have spoken to you, that my joy may be in you, and that your joy may be full.

This is my commandment, that you love one another as I have loved you. Greater love has no man than this, that a man lay down his life for his friends. You are my friends if you do what I command you. No longer do I call you servants, for the servant does not know what his master is doing; but I have called you friends, for all that I have heard from my Father I have made known to you. You did not choose me, but I chose you and appointed you that you should go and bear fruit and that your fruit should abide; so that whatever you ask the Father in my name, he may give it to you. This I command you, to love one another.

John 15:7-17

day 41

Do you keep some friends at arm's reach because you fear being exposed and vulnerable? Are there other friends who you could share anything with? Can you think of one friendship that you want to be intentional about deepening?

day 41

THE PROCESS OF TAMING

Taming by dictionary definition has nothing to do with friendship. Taming means: "To reduce from a wild to a domestic state, to subject to cultivation, to deprive of spirit: humble, subdue." That concept of taming has more to do with superiority/inferiority or even slave/master, a far cry from friendship. That definition may have been what Shakespeare had in mind when he wrote *The Taming of The Shrew*.

The last thing that friendship wants to do is to humble or subdue. To deprive a friend of spirit is the opposite of what support and encouragement in a friendship mean. Friendship celebrates the right of each person to be who he or she is and still be acceptable and loved.

Taming has more to do with intentionality. If you want to be friends, good friends, it will require time and patience. Antoine de Saint-Exupery's *The Little Prince* is a story of taming: "First you will sit down at a little distance from me—like that ... but you will sit a little closer to me, every day."

And slowly but surely a friendship grows because two people enjoy each other, have common interests and goals and are willing to take the time to see their friendship deepen. Otherwise, it will be a relationship of mutual and ritual activities but there will be little growth of intimacy.

Since intimacy scares most of us, we usually settle for less than the deepest friendships. We don't mind some obligations within the relationship, but the depth of commitment and responsibility that is required for a rare friendship is too much. That may be why we can count on one hand the number of our true friends.

There are countless definitions of a friend:

"One who multiplies joys, divides grief."

"One who understands our silence."

"The one who comes in when the whole world has gone out."

Friendships usually begin unintentionally. Two people just discover each other and the joy they have in being together. But enduring friendships endure because of their intentionality. The process of taming each other is entered into with joy as well as trepidation.

The deeper the friendship, the greater is the vulnerability and the exposure to the other person. Baring one's soul before another person is not generally a comfortable feeling. It is even more uncomfortable baring our soul before God, but we have been assured that God is our Friend.

Christians love to sing "What A Friend We Have in Jesus," but we seldom count the cost of what that friendship means. He calls us, even as he called those early disciples. Then comes the process of taming, that process which includes our willingness to listen, to follow, to pray, to be patient, to open ourselves to Him.

Our reward is to hear those wonderful words, "No longer do I call you servants, for the servant does not know what his Master is doing; but I have called you friends, for all that I have heard from my Father I have made known to you." The process of taming is complete.

the salt of the earth, not the honey of the hill day 42

I was ready for him at this point. While he was refilling his pipe, I awkwardly attempted to point out that perhaps after all his insistence didn't quite fit the facts, and this nun who had scrubbed herself to death had nothing in common with 'little choirboys,' little ragamuffins 'who go snivelling around instead of giving orders.'

'Not at all,' he answered rather harshly, 'They've both got the same bee in their bonnets; the only difference is that my little nun had more guts than the ragamuffins. As soon as they come up against it, they start whining that after all the priesthood isn't quite what they imagined, and they chuck it all up. What they want is jam on it. Well, a man can't live on jam, and neither can a Christian society. Our Heavenly Father said mankind was the salt of the earth, not the honey. And our poor world's rather like old man Job, stretched out in all his filth, covered with ulcers and sores. Salt stings on an open wound, but saves you from gangrene. Next to your idea of wiping out the Devil comes that other soft notion of being "loved." Loved for your own sweet selves, of course! A true priest is never loved, get that into your head. And if you must know: the Church doesn't care a rap whether you're loved or not, my lad. Try first to be respected and obeyed. What the Church needs is discipline. You've got to restore order, knowing that disorder will get the upper hand the very next day, because such is the order of things, unluckily: night is bound to turn the day's work upside down—night belongs to the Devil.'

George Bernanos, The Diary Of A Country Priest

The grace of the debonaire is seldom attributed to the Christian in popular imagination. More often than not, the Christian is seen as a dim, spiritless, lackluster personality or an aggressive moral boor. Christians are people who carry the weight of the world on their shoulders. Frequently, according to this popular image, there is more than a slight tinge of masochism to their makeup. They are people who have suffered and denied themselves, and who seem to relish doing so. They are spiritual bleeders, and one can always spot them by the little red badge of humility they wear just over their hearts. Or, if not spiritual bleeders, they are aggressive types on the moral make. They are at pains to witness to their own goodness and the sins of the world. In contradistinction to our Lord's command they always let their right hand know what their left hand is doing. They are the classic American achievers, not in terms of money, sex, or power, but in terms of goodness. But the carefree quality of the debonaire has little in common with either of these types of piety, for both of them are after what the debonaire assume, a sense of significance.

In popular imagination the word "Christian" has fallen on hard times, along with the word "piety." Indeed, a great deal of the time these words are used negatively. A pious person is either a mousy, timid soul or a moral bully and braggart. For many the Christian life is not a lively choice.

Dana Prom Smith, The Debonaire Disciple

You are the salt of the earth; but if the salt has lost its taste, how shall its saltness be restored? It is no longer good for anything except to be thrown out and trodden under foot by men.

Matthew 5:13

If the world hates you, know that it has hated me before it hated you. If you were of the world, the world would love its own; but because you are not of the world, but I chose you out of the world, therefore the world hates you. Remember the word I said to you, "A servant is not greater than his master." If they persecuted me, they will persecute you; if they kept my word, they will keep yours also. But all this they will do to you on my account, because they do not know him who sent me.

John 15:18-20

day 42

Do you ever confuse being loving with being nice? Are there relationships in your life where you need to be a little saltier? Who in your life strikes the perfect balance between salty and sweet?

day 42

THE SALT OF THE EARTH, NOT THE HONEY OF THE HILL

Salt is a god-send! It makes food taste good, it has a healing effect on an open wound, though it does sting, and it also can be used as a preservative. The first time a person is put on a salt-free diet, he or she quickly begins to appreciate salt.

Most of us have experienced people whom we call "the salt of the earth." They are wonderfully stable folk, unassuming, able to laugh at themselves, self-giving, and gracious. They bring zest and flavor to our lives and we are grateful for them; they never seem to lose their savor.

At the other end of the spectrum but still very salty are people we call "old salts." I had an uncle like that. He scandalized his sisters, my aunts and mother, but I loved him. His language was borderline profane; you were never quite sure what he might do next but he was a lot of fun. When he came to visit, he always brought the children a box of candy bars—scandalous! Salty he was, maybe too much so, impious but funny, compassionate, and caring.

Honey is good, even good for you, but it is also sticky and will create gooey gobs of whatever, if not handled carefully. Honey is sweet and runny, so sweet that it is sometimes cloying.

The church is more apt to be honeyed than salty. We prefer to be nice to everyone, to be inclusive of everyone, not to hurt anyone's feelings, for that wouldn't be nice. We want to love everybody and show them how Christian we are. Don't say or do anything that might hurt anyone or demand something of them. Never distinguish better from worse. Be sweet, like Jesus.

Like Jesus! Ha! He who called the Pharisees whited sepulchers, empty tombs, blind guides, hypocrites, blind fools. That is not honey! That's salt! In contemporary pop psychology it is called "tough love." Surely no human being that ever lived was even close to being as sensitive and as loving as Jesus; he gave his life to prove it. But there wasn't a whole lot of honey in the demands he laid on his disciples; the taste of his words was salty.

"Go call your husband," he said to the woman at the well. "I have no husband," she replied. "You have spoken rightly for you have had five husbands." Not a whole lot of honey in that confrontation. Salty! Today we would have done a sociological study and had a psychiatric evaluation before venturing to say anything. Then because she came from a deprived background we would probably have excused everything she had done.

What is it with the church? Again and again we back away from tough decisions because we don't want to hurt anyone's feelings. We take advocacy positions for anything and everything without allowing ourselves the time for tough, salty discussion. We hesitate to question others even when their ideas are deeply questionable.

In the name of compassion we breed incompetence because we find it difficult, if not impossible, to be honest, to face ministers or laymen with what they have done or not done. We have lost the art of speaking the truth in love.

Please pass the salt!

there is no separation day 43

As a writer I have spent so much time trying to bring my dreams to life that, looking back over the years, I remember occasions when life itself seemed dreamlike by comparison. There was the departure of Katherine and Dinah for boarding school, for instance. I knew perfectly well that they were going. We had driven them around to this school and that school till finally they found the one they liked best. And for the whole summer before they left, there was all the talk about it and all the getting ready for it. And when the day finally came, Judy and I drove them there ourselves and met their roommates and lugged endless bags, boxes, and suitcases up endless flights of stairs for them and kissed them goodbye at last, knowing that in a few weeks we would be seeing them again because the school was in Massachusetts and only a couple of hours away, after all. All of this I knew because I had seen it with my own eyes, but there was one thing that I did not see, and it was the most important thing of all.

What I did not see was that even though they were only a couple of hours away, and even though there would be years of weekends and vacations for us to get together whenever we felt like it, there was a sense in which, when we kissed them goodbye that September afternoon, we were kissing them goodbye for keeps. From that day forward, Vermont would never be home for them again in the way it had been. It would be a place to go for weekends and vacations. From that day forward, home, for them, was theirs to find wherever in themselves or in the world they ever happened to find it, if they were lucky enough to find it at all. Two of the four most precious people in my life had left for good, and I had been looking the other way at the time. Life went on, of course, and I managed to get around much as before, but there were times when it felt like trying to get around on broken legs, and there are times when it feels that way still.

It was not just that I greatly missed them but that I feared for them more greatly still. The world does cruel and hurtful things to us all before it's done with us, and with little more to defend themselves against it than their bags full of clothes and their boxes full of rock records, coat hangers, hockey sticks, it was out into that world that they went. The adventures that they have had since are theirs to tell, not mine, but insofar as from time to time the world has worked them over as it works us all over, I have suffered vastly more from such pain as they have known than I have ever suffered from any pain simply of my own...

Frederick Buechner, Now And Then

Very young children, if raised in a kindly environment, are saviors. They know what it is to be helpless, and in the years before they turn to attacking what they fear, they attempt to save. They save by mimicking the earliest acts of love, and in return, expect to be loved. I remained certain, in the face of evidence and experience to the contrary, that my birds, tossed from nests, would grow feathers, fat and wings. I would teach them to fly and they would be mine. I saw no contradiction in that.

But why are four middle-aged adults rounding up chickens as if their own lives depended on it? *We abhor separation* [italics added]. I imagine that each of us, as we search the grounds, is remembering an earlier search for a mother lost on the playground, in a supermarket aisle, between clothing racks in a department store. Memories of loss too early for words and comprehension are the fossil fuels of our mission.

Barbara Lazear Ascher, The Habit Of Loving

When we cry, "Abba! Father!" it is the Spirit himself bearing witness with our spirit that we are children of God, and if children, then heirs, heirs of God and fellow heirs with Christ, provided we suffer with him in order that we may also be glorified with him ... What then shall we say to this? If God is for us, who is against us? ... Who shall separate us from the

day 43

love of Christ? Shall tribulation, or distress, or persecution, or famine, or nakedness, or peril, or sword?

No, in all these things we are more than conquerors through him who loved us. For I am sure that neither death, nor life, nor angels, nor principalities, nor things present, nor things to come, nor powers, nor height, nor depth, nor anything else in all creation, will be able to separate us from the love of God in Christ Jesus our Lord.

Romans 8:15-18, 31, 35, 37-39

For if we have been united with him in a death like his, we shall certainly be united with him in a resurrection like his. We know that our old self was crucified with him so that the sinful body might be destroyed, and we might no longer be enslaved to sin. For he who has died is freed from sin. But if we have died with Christ, we believe that we shall also live with him. For we know that Christ being raised from the dead will never die again; death no longer has dominion over him. The death he died he died to sin, once for all, but the life he lives he lives to God. So you also must consider yourselves dead to sin and alive to God in Christ Jesus.

Romans 6:5-11

day 43

THERE IS NO SEPARATION

A fortnight ago we took our seven-year-old granddaughter to the airport. She had flown all the way from Atlanta by herself to see us. Now she was going home, alone. It was a major experience for her; it was a major experience for her grandparents. In retrospect, it all went well and we are grateful. In prospect, it was a first-time experience for all of us and a bit frightening. Putting her on the plane in the care of the stewardesses and leaving her alone was not easy. The sense of separation was intense and painful.

It was a good illustration for me of a profound truth—the most painful human experience is separation, especially separation from our closest loved ones. We learn this truth early in life when we "spend the night out" for the first time. Sometimes homesickness sets in and we end up going home. Our first time at summer camp is usually a blend of fun and bravado to cover the fact that we miss our home and family.

As we get older, marry, and leave home, we still have our bouts with homesickness. Separation, even when we do not consciously think of it, is not easy. As the years go by the sense of separation intensifies for now we have become familiar with death and, in the normal course of events, have probably lost a friend, relative, or even a parent.

Finally, as we get older and older, death becomes a frequent companion, for not only do we think about it more, but we begin to lose friends and loved ones in increasing numbers. Funerals and memorial services become an unwelcome habit. *C'est la vie!*

The pain of death is found in the sense of loss, in the separation; it seems so final! Death is the end of one with whom we have lived and loved and laughed. The degree of joy in our friend's companionship determines the degree of sorrow in our friend's loss. Often we are decimated! Sometimes it is the end of the flowering before the bloom is complete. Gone! Finished! Kaput!

The most amazing thing about the Christian faith is its affirmation that death is not the end, that in God's love there is no final separation. St. Paul writes these astounding words: "For I am persuaded that neither death, nor life, nor angels, nor principalities, nor powers, nor things present, nor things to come, nor height, nor depth, nor anything else in all creation shall be able to separate us from the love of God in Christ Jesus our Lord." What an affirmation!

I now have reached the wonderful age of 60. It hardly seems possible. It is a startling fact. 60 years of loving and laughing and living with some very special folk, my loved ones, parishioners, and friends. Each time death comes calling the separation seems so final; there is great pain, especially if the departed loved one is young. I can only give comfort as I myself am comforted by that marvelous faith and hope of which Paul writes. "There is no separation..."

THANKS BE TO GOD!

mysterium tremendum day 44

The story is often told of how Heisenberg was struck down by a severe bout of hayfever in May 1925, and went off to recuperate on the rocky island of Heligoland, where he painstakingly tackled the task of interpreting what was known about quantum behavior in these terms. With no distractions on the island, and his hayfever gone, Heisenberg was able to work intensively on the problem. In his autobiographical *Physics and Beyond*, he described his feelings as the numbers began to fall into place, and how at three o'clock one morning he "could no longer doubt the mathematical consistency and coherence of the kind of quantum mechanics to which my calculations pointed. At first, I was deeply alarmed. I had the feeling that, through the surface of atomic phenomena, I was looking at a strangely beautiful interior, and felt almost giddy at the thought that I now had to probe this wealth of mathematical structures nature had so generously spread out before me."

John Gribbin, In Search Of Schrodinger's Cat

Let us consider the deepest and most fundamental element in all strong and sincerely felt religious emotion. Faith unto salvation, trust, love—all these are there. But over and above these is an element which may also on occasion, quite apart from them, profoundly affect us and occupy the mind with a wellnigh bewildering strength. Let us follow it up with every effort of sympathy and imaginative intuition wherever it is to be found, in the lives of those around us, in sudden, strong ebullitions of personal piety and the frames of mind such ebullitions evince, in the fixed and ordered solemnities of rites and liturgies, and again in the atmosphere that clings to old religious monuments and buildings, to temples and to churches. If we do so we shall find we are dealing with something for which there is only one appropriate expression, 'mysterium tremendum'. The feeling of it may at times come sweeping like a gentle tide, pervading the mind with a tranquil mood of deepest worship. It may pass over into a more set and lasting attitude of the soul, continuing, as it were, thrillingly vibrant and resonant, until at last it dies away and the soul resumes its 'profane', non-religious mood of everyday experience. It may burst in sudden eruption up from the depths of the soul with spasms and convulsions, or lead to the strangest excitements, to intoxicated frenzy, to transport, and ecstasy. It has its wild and demonic forms and can sink to an almost grisly horror and shuddering. It has its crude, barbaric antecedents and early manifestations, and again it may be developed into something beautiful and pure and glorious. It may become the hushed, trembling, and speechless humility of the creature in the presence of— whom or what? In the presence of that which is a mystery inexpressible and above all creatures.

Rudolph Otto, The Idea Of The Holy

The world is charged with the grandeur of God.
It will flame out, like shining from shook foil;
It gathers to a greatness, like the ooze of oil
Crushed. Why do men then
now not reck his rod?
Generations have trod, have trod, have trod;
And all is seared with trade;
leared, smeared with toil;
And wears man's smudge and
shares man's smell: the soil
Is bare now, nor can foot feel, being shod.
And for all this, nature is never spent;
There lives the dearest freshness
deep down things;
And though the last lights off
the black West went
Oh, morning, at the brown brink
eastward, springs—
Because the Holy Ghost over the bent
World broods with warm breast
and with ah! bright wings.

Gerald Manley Hopkins, God's Grandeur

day 44

In the year that King Uzziah died I saw the Lord sitting upon a throne, high and lifted up; and his train filled the temple. Above him stood the seraphim; each had six wings: with two he covered his face, and with two he covered his feet, and with two he flew. And one called to another and said:

"Holy, holy, holy is the Lord of hosts;
the whole earth is full of his glory."

And the foundations of the thresholds shook at the voice of him who called, and the house was filled with smoke. And I said, "Woe is me! For I am lost; for I am a man of unclean lips, and I dwell in the midst of a people of unclean lips; for my eyes have seen the King, the Lord of hosts."

Then flew one of the seraphim to me, having in his hand a burning coal which he had taken with tongs from the altar. And he touched my mouth, and said: "Behold, this has touched your lips; your guilt is taken away, and your sin forgiven." And I heard the voice of the Lord saying, "Whom shall I send, and who will go for us?" Then I said, "Here am I! Send me."

Isaiah 6:1-8

day 44

MYSTERIUM TREMENDUM

It was a night over thirty years ago. I was sitting in my car at a high point on the desert floor. The city lights were to the west of me. The mountains to the north and east of me stood out in the bright light of an unbelievably full moon. More than merely radiating, the moon seemed to be spilling its light onto the desert floor like a full cup overflowing. The air was crisp and cool. Saguaros stood like giant sentinels on guard. It was a moment to remember.

I do remember! I was overwhelmed! I was full of awe and wonder and love. It was so beautiful I could hardly take it all in. I could scarcely believe my eyes. I felt small and insignificant, yet I also felt large and at home within the love of God. A very special peace and serenity enfolded me.

The ebullition of which Rudolph Otto speaks and which I felt that night has long since abated. Neither beautiful church nor magnificent cathedral has ever thrilled me as much as that natural cathedral of God did in one glorious moment.

Did it make a difference in my life? Well, yes. It is, I believe, such moments of awe and wonder that lead us to larger moments of service to others. Like Isaiah in the temple we are overwhelmed, cleansed, and opened up to greater possibilities. "Here am I! Send me."

Without such moments of awe and inspiration, would we do as well? I don't think so. The average Christian in the pew is far too intellectual in his response to God. If the ideas are acceptable, he may or may not be moved. This is not a plea for irrationality, but it is a declaration that too few Christians have enough emotional content to their experience of God. Seldom, if ever, have they been moved to the point of exhilaration or ebullience. They have little "idea of the holy."

Correspondingly, they don't make a great effort at being a force for good in the name of God. "Awe-full" experiences shake us out of lethargy, conformity, and doing the same old thing. They challenge, confront, inspire, motivate, and generally change our lives. We need more of them.

It is sad that Christian worship has too often become mundane; sermons fail to inspire. The Sacrament of Holy Communion is more an exercise in necessity than nourishment for the soul. Uplifting, awe-full moments are seldom to be found.

But moments of beauty and awe can also be moments of fear and dread in the presence of God. Isaiah understood that well. "Woe is me for I am a man of unclean lips and I dwell in the midst of a people of unclean lips." He had a beautiful vision but a scary one. His was an awe-full experience of the holy.

Maybe that's our problem. We can stand the beauty but we cannot endure the fear. If "the fear of the Lord is the beginning of wisdom," we prefer to be dumb. Holiness is not to our liking. Much of contemporary Christianity treats God like a "buddy." "He walks with me and He talks with me" and there is nothing to fear. Neither is there any awe, or anything to worship, only ourselves.

It is the *mysterium tremendum* that changes us.

don't neglect the blood day 45

That to love other people is to suffer when they suffer is a truth of life which Christianity recognizes no less than Buddhism does. It is a truth which has much to do, of course, with what the Cross is all about. To say that Christ takes upon himself the sins of the world is to say that he takes upon himself the suffering of the world too. It is to say that in a sense his suffering on the Cross continues for as long as any of us suffers. Furthermore, in being called to take up our own crosses and follow him, we are called to participate in his suffering. But unlike Buddhism, Christianity nevertheless affirms this love that suffers and, what is more, affirms it not in spite of the fact that it suffers but because of it. It affirms it for the reason that to love others to the point of suffering with them and for them in their own suffering is the only way ultimately to heal them, redeem them, if they are to be redeemed at all. It is God's way in Christ, and as we are called to participate with Christ in his suffering, so we are called to be partners with him in his work of redemption. For our own sakes as well as for theirs, we are called to be Christs to all humankind, in other words, and that is close to the heart of our faith and of our lives together as Christians.

Frederick Buechner, Now And Then

There is a fountain filled with blood
Drawn from Immanuel's veins;
And sinners, plunged beneath that flood,
Lose all their guilty stains.
The dying thief rejoiced to see
That fountain in his day;
And there may I, though vile as he,
Wash all my sins away.
Dear dying Lamb, Thy precious blood
Shall never lose its power,
Till all the ransomed Church of God
Be saved, to sin no more.
E'er since by faith I saw the stream
Thy flowing wounds supply,
Redeeming love has been my theme,
And shall be till I die.
When this poor lisping, stamm'ring tongue
Lies silent in the grave,
Then in a nobler, sweeter song,
I'll sing Thy pow'r to save.

William Cowper, There is a Fountain Filled with Blood

Now as they were eating, Jesus took bread, and blessed, and broke it, and gave it to the disciples and said, Take, eat; this is my body." And he took a cup, and when he had given thanks he gave it to them, saying, "Drink of it, all of you; for this is my blood of the covenant, which is poured out for many for the forgiveness of sins. I tell you I shall not drink again of this fruit of the vine until that day when I drink it new with you in my Father's kingdom."

Matthew 26:26-29

And three of the thirty chief men went down, and came about harvest time to David at the cave of Adul'lam, when a band of Philistines was encamped in the valley of Rephaim. David was then in the stronghold; and the garrison of the Philistines was then at Bethlehem. And David said longingly, "O that some one would give me water to drink from the well of Bethlehem which is by the gate!" Then the three mighty men broke through the camp of the Philistines, and drew water out of the well of Bethlehem which was by the gate, and took and brought it to David. But he would not drink of it; he poured it out to the Lord, and said, "Far be it from me, O Lord, that I should do this. Shall I drink the blood of the men who went at the risk of their lives?" Therefore he would not drink of it.

II Samuel 23:13-17

day 45

Have this mind among yourselves, which you have in Christ Jesus, who, though he was in the form of God, did not count equality with God a thing to be grasped, but emptied himself, taking the form of a servant, being born in the likeness of men. And being found in human form he humbled himself and became obedient unto death, even death on a cross. Therefore God has highly exalted him and bestowed on him the name which is above every name, that at the name of Jesus every knee should bow, in heaven and on earth and under the earth, and every tongue confess that Jesus Christ is Lord, to the glory of God the Father.

Philippians 2:5-11

day 45

DON'T NEGLECT THE BLOOD

I was cheerfully biting into a bacon, egg, and cheese sandwich at a fast-food breakfast joint (a terrible habit I am told) when I heard the remark. It came from a man with whom I was familiar by looks and by frequenting the same place. Pastor of a small congregation nearby, he would come there about 7am to drink coffee and do Bible study, spreading his worksheets out on the tables.

I had been careful not to engage him in conversation because the last thing I wanted to discuss while eating my biscuit was Jesus. Hardly communion fare or proper communion setting, so I cared not to discuss our different versions of communion with our Lord. However, a Jehovah's Witness came in and began conversing. The pastor had a beard so they obviously couldn't be close brothers in the faith, but they did rejoice in their mutual salvation in loud celebration. Then came the parting comment from the pastor: "Don't neglect the blood."

I drowned the last bit of cheese and bacon and biscuit with hot coffee and left. The comment, however, would not digest. Though I imagined I knew, I kept wondering what he meant:

"Don't neglect the blood."

Most people I know don't like the subject of blood at all. Drawing blood, giving blood, stopping the flow of blood from an injury, all are to be avoided. Strong men can drop like a stone at the sight of blood. Blood is a vulgar topic.

We have several people in our church community who have never become actual members because of the Sacrament of Communion. They think it is barbaric. Like the Romans' accusation of the early Christians, it is cannibalistic. "Eat his body and drink his blood." Yuck! They refuse to become "communicant members."

The ancient Hebrews, however, weren't so squeamish. They were well acquainted with blood sacrifice. Life and times were difficult and the sight of blood flowing was not unusual or unexpected. If God was appeased by the flow of an animal's blood, they did what they thought was pleasing in God's sight—sacrifice.

At the same time, they respected blood. Blood was synonymous with life. Blood was the source of life. When they gave of their blood, they were giving their life. Nothing has changed! We just don't want to talk about it, until we are faced with surgery; then getting the right kind of blood and safe blood is of vital importance. But until necessary, blood is out of sight, out of mind.

There are lots of pictures of Jesus we like, but not the ones with blood flowing. The shedding of Jesus' blood for our sins is not an easy article of faith unless you are a very conservative Christian. Substitutionary atonement for the Fundamentalist is a no-nonsense doctrine and absolutely essential. "God said it! I believe it! That settles it!" "Don't neglect the blood."

Sacrificial love is still at the heart of life. Countless people, in addition to Jesus, have shed their blood that we might have our freedom and our way of life. Jesus' willingness to sacrifice himself, to pour out his life, is at the heart of our faith.

You may not frequent fast-food breakfast joints, but "Don't neglect the blood."

choosing means renouncing day 46

Choosing also means renouncing. It means defining our person by abandoning resolutely what is not integrated into it by the choice. The intelligence registers everything, turning the person into a kind of limitless museum. It is the will that chooses, and releases the stream of life.

We often see lives that are divided, and paralysed by the division: divided between the dream and the reality, or torn between the conflicting centers of interest. There are many men whose hearts are not in their daily work, which has become to them like a ball and chain dragging at their feet. There are large numbers of women who are divided between a career and family life. There are also not a few who live what one might call provisional lives, in which the choice is constantly postponed. Such people's hearts are not in their present lives, for they are always waiting for the time—which never comes—when their true lives will begin...

But the trouble is that in practice it is not easy to choose between these two roads—between abandoning resolutely one's present life in order to make the life of one's dreams come true, and renouncing the dream in order to throw oneself wholeheartedly into one's present situation. Worst of all is to be unwilling to give up either of them.

Paul Tournier, The Meaning Of Persons

A part of me is quiet. It knows about simplicity, about commitment, and the joy of doing what I do well. That part is the artist, the child—it is receptive and has infinite courage. But time and my busyness drowned the quiet voice.

In the world in which I grew up, more choices meant a better life. It was true for both my parents and my grandparents. I was brought up to believe that the more choices I had, the better.

Never having enough time, I wanted it all, a glutton for new experience. Excited, attracted, distracted, tempted in all directions, I thought I was lucky to have so many choices and I naively believed I could live them all.

A tyranny of lists engulfed me. The lists created the illusion that my life was full.

I would wake at five a.m. eager to begin. The first thing I did was to compose my Things to Do list. This gave me great pleasure, even though the list was nothing more than a superimposed heap of choices, representing all the things I enjoyed doing and all the things I had to do, crowding and bumping against each other. Any organized person would have said, "This is ridiculous. It's unrealistic. No one could accomplish so many things in one day."

Sometimes I would stop in the middle of the day, when the scene on the page looked especially chaotic, and rewrite the list, never thinking to take anything off, but hoping the newly transformed neat rows would overcome my feeling of being overwhelmed. It was a balancing act on one foot—even when I was doing something I enjoyed, my mind jumped about, thinking of what was next on my list.

I never thought to stop and ask myself, "What really matters?" Instead, I gave everything equal weight. I had no way to select what was important and what was not. Things that were important didn't get done, and others, quite unimportant, were completed and crossed off the list.

Accumulating choices was a way of not having to make a choice, but I didn't know that at the time. To eliminate anything was a foreign concept. I felt deprived if I let go of any choices.

Sue Bender, Plain And Simple

People die all the time in their lives. Parts of them die when they make the wrong kind of decision—decisions against life. Sometimes they die bit by bit until finally they are just living corpses walking around. If you are perceptive, you can see it in their eyes; the fire has gone out. Yes, there are a lot of people killed who are living. But you always know when you make a decision against life. When you deny life, you are warned. The cock crows, always, somewhere inside you. The door clicks and you are safe inside—safe and dead.

Anne Morrow Lindberg, The Steep Ascent

day 46

See, I have set before you this day life and good, death and evil. If you obey the commandments of the Lord your God...by loving your God, by walking in his ways, and by keeping his commandments...then you shall live and multiply and the Lord God will bless you... But if your heart turns away, and you will not hear, but are drawn away to worship other Gods and serve them, I declare to you this day, that you shall perish... I call heaven and earth to witness against you this day, that I have set before you life and death, blessing and curse; therefore, choose life, that you and your descendants may live.

Deuteronomy 30:15-20

How long will you go limping with two different opinions? If the Lord is God, follow him; but if Baal, then follow him.

1 Kings 18:21

No one can serve two masters; for either he will hate the one and love the other, or he will be devoted to the one and despise the other. You cannot serve God and Mammon.

Matthew 6:24

I know your works: you are neither cold nor hot. Would that you were cold or hot! So because you are lukewarm, and neither cold nor hot, I will spew you out of my mouth... Behold, I stand at the door and knock; if any one hears my voice and opens the door, I will come in to him and eat with him, and he with me.

Revelation 3:15-16, 20

Jesus said to him, "Friend, why are you here?"

Matthew 26:50

day 46

CHOOSING MEANS RENOUNCING

Most of us understand fully the response of the legendary farmhand who was told to put the big potatoes in one bin and the small potatoes in the other bin. When the farmer came to check on his progress, the farmhand had done nothing. When the farmer asked why he had done nothing, the farmhand replied, "It's the decisions that are hard."

Making choices has never been a human strong point. Most of us will put the choice off until the very last moment; in fact, given the option we will put off the choice until we no longer have to choose. What we fail to accept is that not choosing is a choice. We have a thousand and one excuses for not choosing. To choose one thing is to renounce another, or so it seems. We would rather make our lives inclusive and not have to leave out anything.

Unfortunately, the Bible is filled with choices, ultimate choices from which all other choices flow. A reminder:

"I have set before you life and death... therefore choose life." (Deuteronomy 30:19)

"How long will you go limping with two different opinions? If the Lord is God, follow him; but if Baal, then follow him." (I Kings 18:21)

"No man can serve two masters." (Matthew 6:24)

"Would that you were cold or hot! So because you are lukewarm and neither cold nor hot, I will spew you out of my mouth." (Revelation 3:15)

Renunciation seems like an ugly way to us. We do not like the hard words of Jesus to his mother and brothers, "Who are my mother and my brothers but those who do the will of my Father who is in heaven?" It seems cruel to us to renounce your family. Why can't we have both? Why must we choose?

Most of us try to have things both ways but sometimes it costs us. Many a young person who considers the Christian ministry as a profession has a tough time; their families are against it. Pressure is applied! Choosing Christ over family is too much; they choose other professions. Who knows at what cost to themselves?

Choosing FOR someone may appear to be choosing AGAINST someone else. Affirmation and renunciation are closely related. When a young man falls in love, in order to marry he must choose for his fiancée and against his family. Not really, you say; he can have both. Yes, he can, but trying to maintain both relationships on an equal basis has ruined more than one marriage.

In other cultures where Christianity is not the dominant religion, to choose for Christ is to be exiled from your family. If an Orthodox Jew marries outside his family's faith, he might as well be dead; they hold a funeral service for him. Such exclusiveness seems shocking to us.

Jesus said, "You must deny yourself, take up your cross and follow me." Hard words! Why can't we have it both ways? Because to live is to choose and the hard truth remains: choosing means renunciation as well as affirmation.

the miracle of metamorphosis day 47

The last stop on our tour of the universe brings us back to my home in Princeton. We have descended from sky to earth, from abstract and speculative theories to the world of everyday reality. My youngest daughter came back from a music camp in Massachusetts carrying some Monarch caterpillars in a jar. She found them feeding on milkweed near the camp. We also have milkweed growing in Princeton and so she was able to keep the caterpillars alive. After a few days they stopped feeding, hung themselves up by their tails and began to pupate. The process of pupation is delightful to watch. They squeeze themselves up into the skin of the pupa, like a fat boy wriggling into a sleeping bag that is three sizes too small for him. At the beginning you cannot believe that the caterpillar will ever fit inside, and at the end it turns out that the sleeping bag was exactly the right size.

Two or three weeks later the butterflies emerge. The emergence is even more spectacular than the pupation. Out of the sleeping bag crawls the bedraggled remnant of the caterpillar, much reduced in size and with wet black stubs for wings. Then, in a few minutes, the body dries, the legs and antennae stiffen and the wings unfurl. The bedraggled little creature springs to life as a shimmering beauty of orange and white and black. We set her free in a nearby field and she flies high over the trees, disappearing into the sky. We hope that the move from Massachusetts to Princeton will not have disrupted the pattern of her autumn migration. With luck she will find companions to share with her the long journey to the Southwest. She has a long way to go, most of it against the prevailing winds.

The world of biology is full of miracles, but nothing I have seen is as miraculous as this metamorphosis of the Monarch caterpillar. Her brain is a speck of neural tissue a few millimeters long, about a million times smaller than a human brain. With this almost microscopic clump of nerve cells she knows how to manage her new legs and wings, to walk and to fly, to find her way by some unknown means of navigation over thousands of miles from Massachusetts to Mexico. How can all this be done? How are her behavior patterns programmed first into the genes of the caterpillar and then translated into the neural pathways of the butterfly? These are the mysteries which our biological colleagues are very far from having understood. And yet, we can be confident that we are on the way toward understanding. Progress is rapid in all the necessary disciplines.

Freeman Dyson, Infinite In All Directions

"O you proud Christians,
wretched souls and small,
Who by the dim lights of your twisted minds
Believe you prosper even as you fall,
Can you not see that we are worms, each one
Born to become the angelic butterfly
That flies defenseless to the Judgement Throne."

Dante, Purgatorio

Did you ever think
When a hearse rolls by
That you might be
The next to die?
They wrap you up
In a long white sheet
And throw you down
About fifty feet.
The worms crawl in,
The worms crawl out.
The worms play pinochle
On your snout.
Your tummy turns
A slimy green
And pus rolls out
Just like whip cream.
You sop it up
With a piece of bread
And eat it while
You lie there dead.
The worms crawl in,

day 47

> The worms crawl out.
> The worms play pinochle
> On your snout.
>
> *(A song learned as a youth at Scout Camp)*

But some one will ask, "How are the dead raised? With what kind of body do they come?" You foolish man! What you sow does not come to life unless it dies. And what you sow is not the body which is to be, but a bare kernel, perhaps of wheat or of some other grain. But God gives it a body as he has chosen, and to each kind of seed its own body. For not all flesh is alike, but there is one kind for men, another for animals, another for birds, and another for fish. There are celestial bodies and there are terrestrial bodies; but the glory of the celestial is one, and the glory of the terrestrial is another. There is one glory of the sun, and another glory of the moon, and another glory of the stars; for star differs from star in glory.

So is it with the resurrection of the dead. What is sown is perishable, what is raised is imperishable. It is sown in dishonor, it is raised in glory. It is sown in weakness, it is raised in power. It is sown a physical body, it is raised a spiritual body. If there is a physical body, there is also a spiritual body.

I Corinthians 15:35-44

THE MIRACLE OF METAMORPHOSIS

I once asked a prominent scientist, "What do you think happens when you die?" He proceeded to give me a beautiful theological excursion around all the niceties of resurrection doctrine. When he finished, I said, "Yes, but what do you think happens when you die?" He then said, "Well, I rather think I will be dead, but the discussion is good in that it opens up possibilities for what happens in this world rather than in the next."

His answer was very genuine, but it would not be helpful for those standing around a grave, asking themselves that difficult question of life after death. Or, perhaps his answer would be helpful—he said, "No." At least he was honest, though it took a while to get him there. Surprisingly, there are more Christians who agree with him than we might think.

The New Testament seems to offer the resurrection as proof in the pudding. Supposedly it was all written after the disciples' experiences of seeing Jesus in resurrected form. Only then did they believe and begin to understand what he had been saying to them.

There are those today who think we can hold on to Jesus and the faith without necessarily believing in his resurrection. I doubt that! If the church and its members do not hold to the resurrection, I believe we will fade from the scene. The resurrection is the greatest miracle and our greatest hope. The church is built on the disciples' experience of resurrection.

We live in a world looking for something to hope in and for. It is the resurrection that offers hope of change, in this world (as the scientist hoped for) and in the next. Would the change occur in this world without the hope of change in the next? I doubt it. Hope in something beyond buttresses our faith in trying to change the world about us. It is possible to demythologize people straight into despair.

I have sat in Pacific Grove, California, and watched hundreds of Monarch butterflies in a tree, thousands of them in the area. The citizens there hold an annual festival to honor their return. How beautiful they are as they waft their way through the summer air. They weren't always so lovely, however, having gone through a miraculous change, a metamorphosis from cocooned pupa to magnificent winged creature. Now, they are a lovely image of resurrection possibility.

Metamorphosis according to the *Oxford American Dictionary* means "a change of form or character." If God can work that miracle with the Monarch butterfly, why not with us? Some scientists believe that in time we will understand the process of butterfly metamorphosis. Perhaps, but that won't change the miracle that there are such creatures of beauty.

Jesus, too, was changed and when they saw Him, they were changed. As God's Spirit works in those of us who believe, we, too, are changed. That change in our present life is a precursor to a more profound change that comes at our death: "in a flash, in the twinkling of an eye, we shall all be changed." The language may be metaphorical but the change is for real, another miracle of metamorphosis.

Let us rejoice!

the denizens of the night day 48

Sleep is surely one of God's most precious gifts, as none know better than those who are victims of insomnia. It has been ordained that our lives here below should consist in an alteration of activity and rest, of sleeping and waking; but we could not support the activity if we had no rest, or the waking hours if we had no sleep. How blessed a thing it is, then, that we are not expected to retain the conscious control of our lives by night as well as by day, but that we are allowed to lay the reins in God's hands, entrusting ourselves to His care when we are least able to care for ourselves. But we must really entrust ourselves. Sleep comes best to those who most put their trust in God. That is what the Psalmist means by saying, "He giveth his beloved sleep." His beloved are those who trust Him. There is no better soporific than a trustful heart, no surer way of having a good night's rest than to commend ourselves to God's keeping, in believing prayer, before we go to sleep. Of course some men and women are constitutionally light sleepers. Insomnia may be due to any one of several different causes. But if the commonest cause of it is a mind unrelaxed from care, its best cure is to cast all our cares upon the Keeper of Israel who neither slumbers nor sleeps. Elizabeth Barrett Browning is not much read nowadays, but perhaps no poem of hers is better remembered than the one that begins with the verse:

> Of all the thoughts of God that are
> Borne inward unto souls afar,
> Along the Psalmist's music deep,
> Now tell me if that any is,
> For gift or grace, surpassing this—
> 'He giveth His beloved, sleep.'

John Baillie, Christian Devotion

> They come in a variety of forms—
> those denizens of the night.
> Violence, pestilence, and storms—
> Weird dreams
> wake me. Uptight!
> Late for funeral, wedding or church
> Some poor
> parishioner left in the lurch.
> Regularly does that anxiety devil
> Haunt my dreams in his revel.
> Stomach pain—has cancer come?
> What a way to be taken "home"?
> Child in trouble? What to do
> Can occupy a night or two.
> Caught behind the enemies' lines,
> A harrowing escape lies through the mines.
> If you've ever been surrounded by the "mob,"
> It's enough to make you sob.
> By daylight I am a peaceful soul;
> In my sleep violence takes its toll.
> According to Freud the cause is my Id
> When the Superego removes the lid.
> I, for myself, cannot discern
> Why in the night I toss and turn.
> Faith can conquer things by light,
> But beware the denizens of the night.

Samuel Johnson Lindamood

> Weary with toil, I haste me to my bed
> The dear repose for limbs with travel tired;
> But then begins a journey in my head
> To work my mind, when body's work's expir'd:
> For then my thoughts—from far where I abide—
> Intend a zealous pilgrimage to thee,
> And keep my drooping eyelids open wide,
> Looking on darkness which the blind do see:
> Save that my soul's imaginary sight
> Presents thy shadow to my sightless view,
> Which, like a jewel hung in ghastly night,
> Makes black night beauteous and her old face new.
> Lo! thus, by day my limbs, by night my mind,
> For thee, and for myself no quiet find.

Shakespeare, Sonnet 27

day 48

I will both lay me down in peace and sleep:
for thou, Lord, only makest me dwell in safety.

Psalm 4:8 (KJV)

Unless the Lord builds the house,
those who build it labor in vain.
Unless the Lord watches over the city,
the watchman stays awake in vain.
It is in vain that you rise up early and go late to rest,
eating the bread of anxious toil;
for he gives to his beloved sleep.

Psalm 127:1-2

And when he got into the boat, his disciples followed him. And behold, there arose a great storm on the sea, so that the boat was being swamped by the waves; but he was asleep. And they went and woke him, saying, "Save, Lord; we are perishing." And he said to them, "Why are you afraid, O men of little faith?" Then he rose and rebuked the winds and the sea; and there was a great calm. And the men marveled, saying, "What sort of man is this, that even winds and sea obey him?"

Matthew 8:23-27

Then Jesus, crying with a loud voice, said, "Father, into thy hands I commit my Spirit."

Luke 23:46

day 48

THE DENIZENS OF THE NIGHT

The world is divided into two kinds of people: those who sleep with a night light and those who don't. I do! Always have! Always will! The world is also divided into those who sleep well and those who don't. I don't! My father died a long, slow death. I remember lying awake and hearing more than I should.

I'm lucky, however. I don't suffer from insomnia. I'm just not a good sleeper. Sometimes it's because I eat and drink too much; mostly it's because my mind wants to worry and think too much. Sleep research has helped. I realize now that I will not pass out the next day or even be overly tired if I can just relax and lie there.

There's the rub! Ethereal and unreal forms during the day seem to take on substance at night. Pain is worse, much worse at night. The peculiar demons of the previous day and the anticipated ones of tomorrow cavort with glee in their greater capacity to torture poor souls at night.

What to do? We could start a Society Of Sleepless Ones (SOSO) with a hot line to call on especially bad nights when the demons are going crazy, as is the sleepless one. Fellow-sufferers abound when the problem is confessed openly. Common problems bind us together, but the wee hours of morning are a poor time to call another sufferer who might be sleeping for a change. SOSO could not survive on merely sharing sleep problems at dinner parties or church socials. Like members of Alcoholics Anonymous, we would need to share our mutual burden—but it's the wrong time of day, or rather night.

Therapists, like the above-mentioned demons, rub their hands with glee at the sound of our voices. There is an incredible amount of therapeutic process and unimaginable dollars behind those crazy things that go flying through our heads at night. Telling some therapists your dreams is like watching small children in a candy shop. They salivate!

Some fellow Christians tell me they repeat scripture, like the 23rd Psalm, until they go to sleep. It's a religious way of counting sheep. I jest, but I just don't think recitation of scripture, even the 23rd Psalm, makes sleep come that easy, especially for charter members of SOSO.

Psalm 4:8 is of great comfort to me: "I will both lay me down in peace, and sleep; for thou, Lord, only makest me dwell in safety."

Therein lies a commitment to the God whom we believe to be the context of our lives. Nothing less than a faith which looks to a God who undergirds us, not only in life but also in death, not only in waking but also in sleeping, is going to help.

I suspect that my own personal demons will not suddenly disappear as I remind myself of that faith about 3 a.m. (No wonder we refer to it as an ungodly hour. It is!) But during the struggle of the soul it is comforting to say, "Into thy hands do I commend my spirit." The night belongs to God also.

"Now I lay me down to sleep,

I pray thee, Lord, my soul to keep."

But just in case, turn on the night light.

when you can't find the tiger day 49

I have a friend whose only tool on an archeological dig along the Dead Sea was a number-eight pure bristle paintbrush. "We were digging for the foundations of an ancient civilization, but we weren't allowed to dig," she tells me. "We were only allowed to gently brush away the sand lest we destroy what we might find buried there." For weeks my friend sat beneath a scorching desert sun, sifting sand until she uncovered columns that had supported a temple.

As I enter middle age I feel that I too am in the desert, brushing away sand in search of my own foundations. Delicately, so as not to destroy that which I might find there. Delicately, so as not to destroy that which holds me. Unlike raucous, earlier years of building up and taking down and building up again with the devil-may-care enthusiasm of children at the beach, these are painstaking times. What we hope to uncover are ourselves.

If old age is a time of summing up, then middle age is a time of taking stock. A time of paying heed to matters of the heart, to the consequences of our loving and passions. It is a time of looking back at what we were, out at the world around us and into ourselves and those closest to us to determine what really matters. To discard what does not. I have come to wonder whether this is not some natural order that facilitates a more full-spirited, less heavily burdened journey to the end.

It's a time of knowing love well enough to learn its ultimate lesson: that life is a bit of a cheat. That with love there is never enough time. That without it, there is not time at all.

Barbara Lazear Ascher, The Habit Of Loving

For many Americans, especially men, success is identified with work. It's ironic that we get a classic statement of the Protestant work ethic from a Jew, Arthur Miller. He said one time, "I'm not happy in the sense that there are no problems but I'm always happy if I'm working. I'm a person who has never known how to take a vacation so all life is either work or a preparation for it. To be fruitful is to be happy. You don't have to feel you've got the tiger by the tail. It's when you can't find the tiger that the agony begins.

I sense a quiet agony among many people who can't find the tiger and who are out looking for the tiger, and who will admit that having 'made it,' they haven't 'got it made.' People who are on the make for a little more meaning in their lives..."

Years ago I came across a book called *The Middle Age Crisis* by Barbara Fried. As I read it, I kept thinking, "How does she understand me? How does she know what's going on in me?" The wit and wisdom of the book were a delight and comfort to me. The author quoted one woman as saying to a counselor, "Everything that makes life worth living is either turning gray, drying up or leaving home." A man said, "I've got some kind of free-floating itch I can't possibly get my fingers on to scratch."

Robert A Raines, Success Is A Moving Target

Therefore, I tell you, do not be anxious about your life, what you shall eat or what you shall drink, nor about your body, what you shall put on. Is not life more than food, and the body more than clothing? Look at the birds of the air: they neither sow nor reap nor gather into barns, and yet your heavenly Father feeds them. Are you not of more value than they? And which of you by being anxious can add one cubit to his span of life? And why are you anxious about clothing? Consider the lilies of the field, how they grow; they neither toil nor spin; yet I tell you, even Solomon in all his glory was not arrayed like one of these. But if God so clothes the grass of the field, which today is alive and tomorrow is thrown into the oven, will he not much more clothe you, O men of little faith? Therefore do not be anxious, saying, 'What shall we eat?' or 'What shall we drink?' or 'What shall we wear?' For the Gentiles seek all these things; and your heavenly Father knows that you need them all. But seek first his kingdom and his righteousness, and all these things shall be yours as well. Therefore, do not be anxious about tomorrow, for tomorrow will be anxious for itself. Let the day's own trouble be sufficient for the day.

Matthew 6:25-34

day 49

WHEN YOU CAN'T FIND THE TIGER

Having been raised in the desert, I love the imagery of using a paintbrush to slowly and carefully brush away the sands that obscure sight. Searching for one's self demands great patience or one may wipe away something precious, never to be recovered. The sands of time that cover our memories need painstaking archeology.

At age sixty I can scarcely claim to be middle-aged, but I still have those feelings. "You don't have to feel you've got the tiger by the tail. It's when you can't find the tiger that the agony begins."

Having control over our lives is very important. When we lose control, we become anxious, even afraid. When the sands have obscured the tiger, we agonize indeed, and are apt to pick up a shovel instead of a paintbrush. Surely we can dig our way out. Probably, but a paint brush is better. As I have brushed away the sand looking for foundations, some ancient truths have emerged. When you can't find the tiger:

1-You turn inside rather outside. The biggest problem we have is that we cannot escape ourselves. Any attempt to run from the problem will not help because we take ourselves wherever we go. The problem is not geographical.

Who are we? What's inside us? What kind of a grade do we give ourselves? Personal worth is inside, not outside. "If a person is in Christ, he or she is a new creation." Our greatest sense of worth comes from believing that God accepts us. Christ died for us, for me. "If God be for us, who can be against us?" A sense of personal worth flows from acceptance of those beliefs. Martin Luther, in bad moments, would go around muttering to himself, "Eo baptismo, eo baptismo" (I am baptized, I am baptized).

2-You learn to subtract rather than add. Most of us find ourselves in situational madness--kids, finances, parents, job security, community responsibilities, to name only a few. We have to learn anew "how unimportant the unimportant really is."

Henry David Thoreau's advice was to simplify, simplify. The idea was not original with him. The words of Jesus seem absolutely out-of-date and impossible, don't they? "Why are you anxious...?" Well, actually for a lot of reasons, and ridding ourselves of those reasons is hard, hard, hard.

We must learn our own form of "new math." Subtract! Do away with, get rid of, say no to. All those phrases come to mind easily but not to mouth well. "NO!" It's a difficult word to use when we really need it.

3-You risk rather than retreat. As hard as it may be, it is more important to be open than closed, to be vulnerable rather than defensive, to be exposed to pain rather than protected from it. Kahlil Gibran wrote, "Your pain is the breaking of the shell that encloses your understanding."

When you can't find the tiger, go for it, don't back away. Life is too short to become self-protective and isolated. Some other words of Jesus come through the swirling dust, "For whoever would save his life will lose it; and whoever loses his life for my sake and the gospel's, will save it."

beyond astonishment **day 50**

In the sixth month the angel Gabriel was sent from God to a city of Galilee named Nazareth, to a virgin betrothed to a man whose name was Joseph, of the house of David; and the virgin's name was Mary. And he came to her and said, "Hail, O favored one, the Lord is with you!" But she was greatly troubled at the saying, and considered in her mind what sort of greeting this might be. And the angel said to her, "Do not be afraid, Mary, for you have found favor with God. And behold, you will conceive in your womb and bear a son, and you shall call his name Jesus.

> He will be great, and will be called
> the Son of the Most High;
> and the Lord God will give to him the
> throne of his father David,
> and he will reign over the house of Jacob for ever;
> and of his kingdom there will be no end."

And Mary said to the angel, "How shall this be, since I have no husband?" And the angel said to her,

> "The Holy Spirit will come upon you,
> and the power of the Most High will overshadow you;
> therefore the child to be born will be called holy,
> the Son of God.

And behold, your kinswoman Elizabeth in her old age has also conceived a son; and this is the sixth month with her who was called barren. For with God nothing will be impossible." And Mary said, "Behold, I am the handmaid of the Lord; let it be to me according to your word." And the angel departed from her.

Luke 1:26-38

Now the birth of Jesus Christ took place in this way. When his mother Mary had been betrothed to Joseph, before they came together she was found to be with child of the Holy Spirit; and her husband Joseph, being a just man and unwilling to put her to shame, resolved to divorce her quietly. But as he considered this, behold, an angel of the Lord appeared to him in a dream, saying, "Joseph, son of David, do not fear to take Mary your wife, for that which is conceived in her is of the Holy Spirit; she will bear a son, and you shall call his name Jesus, for he will save his people from their sins." All this took place to fulfil what the Lord had spoken by the prophet: "Behold, a virgin shall conceive and bear a son, and his name shall be called Emmanuel" (which means, God with us). When Joseph woke from sleep, he did as the angel of the Lord commanded him; he took his wife, but knew her not until she had borne a son; and he called his name Jesus.

Matthew 1:18-25.

And what more shall I say? For time would fail me to tell of Gideon, Barak, Samson, Jepthah, of David and Samuel and the prophets—who through faith conquered kingdoms, enforced justice, received promises, stopped the mouths of lions, quenched raging fire, escaped the edge of the sword, won strength out of weakness, became mighty in war, put foreign armies to flight. Women received their dead by resurrection. Some were tortured, refusing to accept release, that they might rise again to a better life. Others suffered mocking and scourging, and even chains and imprisonment. They were stoned, they were sawn in two, they were killed with the sword; they went about in skins of sheep and goats, destitute, afflicted, ill-treated—of whom the world was not worthy—wandering over deserts and mountains, and in dens and caves of the earth.

And all these, though well attested by their faith, did not receive what was promised, since God had foreseen something better for us, that apart from us they should not be made perfect.

Hebrews 11:32-40

day 50

Do you feel paralyzed or bewildered about anything in your life? Is there something you feel called to do but you're afraid to try because you don't believe success is possible?

day 50

BEYOND ASTONISHMENT

Webster defines astonish: "To stun, paralyze, deaden; to stupefy the mind, to bewilder or daze." I read a survey in which sixty percent of the astonished New Yorkers polled said they would rather live elsewhere. Crime, corruption, violence, drugs, and craziness of activity are just a few of the causes.

New York City is not alone. We live in a world where so many crazy things happen every day that most of us are stupefied. Outrageous international power grabs, stunning national politics, the sheer scale of corporate greed, the recurrent possibility of war. Yes! We are bewildered. We ask ourselves, "How bad can things get?" "How much can we take?" Who knows? We are astonished!

The birth of Jesus had its own degree of astonishment. Mary must have been slightly bewildered when the angel made THE ANNOUNCEMENT, but think of Joseph when she told him. Pregnancy is one thing, but hallucinations are another. Thanks to his own dream Joseph hangs in there but what a nine months that must have been—confused, bewildered.

Then there was the extended donkey trip at the time of Mary's deliverance—no choice, the government ordered it. The Holiday Inns were all filled and they had to improvise. Jesus was born and then, more astonishment. Shepherds from the fields showed up (slightly different looking and smelling than the ones in traditional pageants). Then foreigners from afar came, bearing gifts, including embalming spices, no less. And finally Herod's decree meant they dare not go home again. Beyond astonishment!

Surely there is a time for legitimate withdrawal, for quitting, for saying, "Enough!" "I, R.D. Jones, no longer have a sewing machine. I smashed it." "I, Mary, have had enough. I'm staying in Egypt." "I, John Doe, am sick of it. I want out. I quit!" "Cheer up," we say, "things could be worse." AND THEY ARE WORSE! Do we have a legitimate right to quit? To throw in the towel? To come unglued? To resign from the human race? Possibly, but the real question is do we choose to do so?

Mary and Joseph chose to believe that God meant what he said, that God would be present with them and help them survive. The Book of Hebrews says, "Time fails me to tell of Gideon, Samson, Barak, Jepthath." The writer tells a story of people who survived, not only survived but lived with spirit and courage. The early Christians, according to the book of Acts, "turned the world upside-down." They moved beyond astonishment!

The Bible insists that we are custodians of a new birth (Christmas), of rebirth and resurrection (Easter), and the possibility of creating a new world. That's what the church is all about. We are a community that testifies that it is possible to move beyond astonishment.

We may not turn the world upside-down but we can keep going, refusing to quit. We can choose to believe what God has done for us in Jesus Christ and what God calls us to do through the power of the Spirit. We can choose to believe that God will keep the divine promises, that God will be with us and help us survive. Not only can we survive but we, too, can live with spirit and courage, moving on, beyond astonishment.

acknowledgements

My partners in this project are first and foremost Gay and Doug Lane. Gay was Sam's close friend and co-worker for many years. Together, Gay and Doug generously funded this volume. Sam's beloved wife, Ann Lindamood Fischer, has given her blessing to this project. She and the four children she raised with Sam—Robin, Wendy, Peggy, and Missy—share our desire that it should help its readers as well as honor their late husband and father. My son, Ben, worked on photography, and I have included some of his photographs to illustrate the daily themes. Ben was too young to know Sam, but Sam baptized him as a baby and Ben has come to know something of Sam's spirit through this book. I think readers will have the same experience. I am grateful to Larry Whitney, Kate Stockly, Matthew Beal, and Dave Rohr for valiant editorial help. Dave was magnificent in handling the nightmare of securing permissions; I doubt that we would have reached the end if it weren't for his dedication and organizational skills. Finally, I'm glad to acknowledge Melody Stanford Martin of Cambridge Creative Group for her design and publication expertise, and Karen Campbell from Karen Campbell Media for her publicity work.

— Wesley J. Wildman

index of readings

THE FORTY DAYS OF LENT

A Prayer to Begin - "Listen, Lord - A Prayer" from GOD'S TROMBONES by James Weldon Johnson, copyright 1927 by Penguin Random House LLC, renewed 1955 by Grace Nail Johnson. Used by permission of Viking Books, an imprint of Penguin Publishing Group, a division of Penguin Random House LLC. All rights reserved.

Day 1 - Repetitive Regrets
- "As If Innocence Had Ever Been" — from Holy the Firm by Annie Dillard. Copyright (c) 1977 by Annie Dillard. Used by permission of HarperCollins Publishers.
- A General Confession — Book of Common Prayer
- Psalm 51:1-5, Psalm 103:8-12
- Romans 7:15,21,24, I John 1:8-9, II Corinthians 5:17
- Reflection

Day 2 - What Is Real?
- "What Is Real?" — Margery Williams, *The Velveteen Rabbit*, Doubleday and Company, Inc., New York, 1971, pp. 16-20.
- "Who In The World Am I?" — Lewis Carroll, *Alice's Adventure In Wonderland*
- "That I Am A Man" — Master Eckhart, *Fragments*
- "I Think I Could Turn And Live With Animals" — Walt Whitman
- John 1:12, I John 4:7-17a
- Reflection

Day 3 - Running Away From It All
- "The Anxiety of the Runner" — Copyright © 1979 by the Christian Century. "The Anxiety of the Runner: Terminal Helplessness" by D. William Faupel is reprinted by permission from the Aug.29-Sept. 5, 1979 issue of the Christian Century. All rights reserved.
- Psalm 139:7-8, 11-12; Luke 14:15-24, Philippians 2:14-16, 3:12-14
- Reflection

Day 4 - The Meaning Of Persons
- "The Meaning of Persons" from The Meaning of Persons by Paul Tournier. Translated by Edwin Hudson. Copyright (c) 1957 by Paul Tournier, renewed (c) 1985 SCM Press Ltd. Used by permission of HarperCollins Publishers.
- As You Like It — William Shakespeare
- John 1:12-13, John 3:1-8, Mark 8:34-37
- Reflection

Day 5 - Loneliness
- "The Wound of Loneliness" —Excerpt(s) from THE WOUNDED HEALER: MINISTRY IN CONTEMPORARY SOCIETY by Henri J. M. Nouwen, copyright © 1972 by Henri J. M. Nouwen. Copyright renewed © 2000 by Sue Mosteller, Executrix of the Estate of Henri J. M. Nouwen. Used by permission of Doubleday, an imprint of the Knopf Doubleday Publishing Group, a division of Penguin Random House LLC. All rights reserved.
- "Returning To The Sea" — Sheldon B. Kopp, *If You Meet The Buddha On The Road, Kill Him!*, Bantam Books, New York, 1972, pp. 206-210. Used by permission of Science and Behavior Books, Inc. All rights reserved.
- "All man's history is an endeavor to shatter his loneliness" — Excerpt(s) from MODERN MAN IS OBSOLETE by Norman Cousins, copyright 1945 renewed © 1972 by Norman Cousins. Used by permission of Viking Books, an imprint of Penguin Publishing Group, a division of Penguin Random House LLC. All rights reserved.
- Matthew 27:45-50
- Reflection

Day 6 - Check Your Escalator
- *The Confessions of Saint Augustine* - Saint Augustine
- Excerpt from "The Hollow Men" from COLLECTED POEMS 1909-1962 by T.S. Eliot. Copyright © 1925 by Houghton Mifflin Harcourt Publishing Company, renewed 1953 by Thomas Stearns Eliot. Reprinted by permission of Houghton Mifflin Harcourt Publishing Company. All rights reserved.
- Acts 9:1-9, Acts 28:27, Romans 10:8-10, Mark 1:14-20, Matthew 18:1-4
- Reflection

index of readings

Day 7 - The Awesome Nature of Freedom
- Genesis 4:6-8
- "Making Your Own Freedom" – from Pulling Your Own Strings by Wayne W. Dyer. Copyright(c) 1978 by Wayne W. Dyer. Used by permission of HarperCollins Publishers.
- From ZORBA THE GREEK by Nikos Kazantzakis. Copyright © 1953 by Simon & Schuster, Inc.; renewed 1981 by Simon & Schuster, a division of Gulf & Western Corporation. Reprinted with the permission of Simon & Schuster, Inc. All rights reserved.
- John 8:31-35, Mark 14:3-9
- Reflection

Day 8 - Believing Impossible Things
- "Believing Six Impossible Things Before Breakfast" – Lewis Carroll, Alice In Wonderland, Grosset and Dunlap, United States of America, 1986, pps 221, 222.
- "Christian Agnosticism" – Leslie D. Weatherhead, The Christian Agnostic, Abingdon Press, New York, 1965, p. 2.
- "The Son Of God" – Westminster Confession, Chapter VIII
- Colossians 1:14-20
- Reflection

Day 9 - Some People Are More Equal Than Others
- "Some Animals Are More Equal" – Excerpt from ANIMAL FARM by George Orwell. Copyright © 1946 by Houghton Mifflin Harcourt Publishing Company and renewed 1974 by Sonia Brownell Orwell. Reprinted by permission of Houghton Mifflin Harcourt Publishing Company. All rights reserved.
- "We Hold These Truths' – Declaration of Independence
- John 8:32, I John 4:13-21
- Reflection

Day 10 - The Lusts That Drive Us
- "The Monsters Inhabiting Our Heads" – Excerpt(s) from BREAKFAST OF CHAMPIONS: A NOVEL by Kurt Vonnegut, copyright © 1973 and copyright renewed 2002 by Kurt Vonnegut, Jr. Used by permission of Dell Publishing, an imprint of Random House, a division of Penguin Random House LLC. All rights reserved.
- Matthew 12:43-45
- Psalm 81:12 (KJV), Proverbs 6:25 (KJV)
- Galatians 5:16-17 (NKJV), I John 2:16-17 (NKJV), Acts 3:4-6
- Reflection

Day 11 - Different Strokes For Different Folks
- "Our age is retrospective" - Ralph Waldo Emerson, Nature, James Munroe and Company, Boston and Cambridge, 1836.
- "Varieties of Religious Experience" – William James, Varieties Of Religious Experience, Random House, New York, 1902, pp. 476-478.
- Psalm 145:3
- Selections From Job: Job 36:26, 37:5, 11:7-8, 5:6-9
- Acts 17:22-32
- Reflection

Day 12 - Crap-Detecting
- "Who knows himself a braggart" - All's Well That Ends Well, William Shakespeare
- Jeremiah 17:9-10; Hebrews 4:12-13; Matthew 6:1-6
- Luke 12:1-3; Ephesians 4:11-16; 1 John 4:1-2
- Reflection

Day 13 - A Simple Notion of Being Good
- "Standeth God Within The Shadow" – James Russell Lowell
- Romans 5:6-8
- "Is Loving Banal?" – from Plain and Simple by Sue Bender. Copyright (c) 1989 by Sue Bender. Used by permission of HarperCollins Publishers.
- Matthew 18:1-6,10, Matthew 19:13-15; Matthew 25:31-40
- Reflection

Day 14 - No Man Is an Island
- "No Man Is An Island" – John Donne
- "There Is A Destiny" – Edwin Markham
- "Balancing Solitude And Community" – Excerpt(s) from GIFT FROM THE SEA by Anne Morrow Lindbergh, copyright © 1955, 1975, copyright renewed 1983 by Anne Morrow Lindbergh. Used by permission of Pantheon Books, an imprint of

index of readings

the Knopf Doubleday Publishing Group, a division of Penguin Random House LLC. All rights reserved.
- Ecclesiastes 4:8-12; Matthew 18:19-20; I Corinthians 12:12-27
- Reflection

Day 15 - Ready To Go
- "Live we how we can, yet die we must" - Shakespeare, *Henry the VI*
- "Soar We Now" – Charles Wesley
- 1 Thessalonians 4:13-14; Matthew 24:40-44; John 12:24-25
- Reflection

Day 16 - What Is Love?
- "Love Is A Person" – Madeleine L'Engle, *A Circle Of Quiet*, A Fawcett Crest Book, Greenwich, Conn., 1972, p. 64. Used by permission of Levine, Plotkin, and Menin, LLP.
- "Love Is Not A Feeling" – From THE ROAD LESS TRAVELED by M. Scott Peck, M.D. Copyright © 1978 M. Scott Peck. Reprinted with the permission of Touchstone, a division of Simon & Schuster, Inc. All rights reserved.
- "What is Love?" - Erich Fromm, *Man for Himself*, Rinehart and Company, New York, 1947, pp. 129-130. Used by permission of Henry Holt and Company and Macmillan Publishing. All rights reserved.
- I Corinthians 13:4-8a, John 15:12-17
- Reflection

Day 17 - Searchers
- "Searchers" – James Kavanaugh, *There Are Men Too Gentle To Live Among Wolves*, Nash Publishing, Los Angeles, 1970, Preface. Used by permission of Cathy Kavanaugh and The James Kavanaugh Institute. All rights reserved.
- "More things in heaven and earth" - Shakespeare, *Hamlet*
- Psalm 8, Isaiah 55:6-7; Ecclesiastes 2:9-11; Joel 2:28
- Matthew 7:7-8; I Corinthians 13:12
- Reflection

Day 18 - The Best Things In The Worst Times
- Ecclesiastes 3:1-8; 1 Kings 19:9-18; Galatians 5:9-10, II Corinthians 4:7-12
- Reflection

Day 19 - Finding Meaning Under Any Circumstances
- "The Last Of Our Freedoms" – "Man's Search for Meaning" by Viktor E. Frankl Copyright ©1959, 1962, 1984, 1992, 2006 by Viktor E. Frankl Reprinted by permission of Beacon Press, Boston
- "The Clue To Our Irreligion" – Reinhold Niebuhr, *Leaves From The Notebook Of A Tamed Cynic*, Meridian Books, New York, 1957, pp. 79-80. Used by permission of Westminster John Knox Press. All rights reserved.
- Isaiah 53:4-7
- Matthew 7: 24-27; Matthew 27:11-14
- Reflection

Day 20 - The Therapy Of Breadbaking
- "Breadbaking" – Excerpt(s) from THE LAUREL'S KITCHEN BREAD BOOK by Laurel Robertson, Carol Flinders and Bronwen Godfrey, copyright © 1984, 2003 by The Blue Mountain Center of Meditation, Inc.. Used by permission of Random House, an imprint and division of Penguin Random House LLC. All rights reserved.
- Matthew 4:3-4, Matthew 6:11, John 6:30-35,48-51,
- Matthew 26:26-29; I Corinthians 5:6-8
- Reflection

Day 21 - You Can't Go Home Again
- "Faith Involves Leaving Home" – Robert A. Raines, *Going Home*, Harper and Row, San Francisco, 1979, pp. 28-30.
- Numbers 13:30-14:4; Deuteronomy 6:4-9
- Luke 9:57-62, John 20:10
- Reflection

Day 22 - Lip-Smacking, Exuberant Delight
- "The Excesses of God" – Excerpt from *Robinson Jeffers: Dimensions of a Poet*, Fordham University Press, 1995. Used by permission of Fordham University Press. All rights reserved.
- "Pied Beauty" – Gerald Manley Hopkins
- Genesis 1:26-31; Psalm 19:1-4
- Matthew 11:16-19
- Reflection

index of readings

Day 23 – Facing Your Mortality
- "Finding Strength in Love" – Peter Findlay, Copyright © 1983 by the Christian Century. Reprinted by permission from the October 26, 1983 issue of the Christian Century. All rights reserved.
- "For within the hollow crown" – Shakespeare, *Richard III*
- Psalm 23: 1-4; Psalm 90:10, 12, 17
- John 11:25-26; Romans 8:38-39; James 4:13-16
- Reflection

Day 24 – Single-Minded Not Narrow-Minded
- "Single Minded Not Narrow Minded" – Excerpt(s) from THE GENESEE DIARY: REPORT FROM A TRAPPIST MONASTERY by Henri Nouwen, copyright © 1976 by Henri J. M. Nouwen. Copyright renewed © 2004 by Sue Mosteller, CSJ, executrix of the Estate of Henri J.M. Nouwen Used by permission of Doubleday, an imprint of the Knopf Doubleday Publishing Group, a division of Penguin Random House LLC. All rights reserved.
- James 1:5-8, Philippians 1:12-21
- Reflection

Day 25 – Euphoric Euthanasia
- "To be, or not to be" – Shakespeare, *Hamlet*
- "The Naturalness Of Death" – Excerpt(s) from LIVES OF A CELL by Lewis Thomas, copyright © 1974 by Lewis Thomas; copyright © 1971, 1972, 1973 by Massachusetts Medical Society. Used by permission of Viking Books, an imprint of Penguin Publishing Group, a division of Penguin Random House LLC. All rights reserved.
- Job 14:1-14
- Luke 23:44-46; I Thessalonians 4:13-18
- Reflection

Day 26 – There Is Hope In A Burp
- Genesis 11:1-9; Proverbs 11:2-4; Isaiah 2:12-17
- 1 Corinthians 1:22-29; Philippians 2:1-11; James 1:9-11
- Reflection

Day 27 – Dealing With The Absurd
- "Catch 22" – From CATCH-22 by Joseph Heller. Copyright © 1955, 1961 by Joseph Heller. Copyright renewed © 1989 by Joseph Heller. Reprinted with the permission of Simon & Schuster, Inc. All rights reserved.
- "The Organization of The Absurd" – from Tomorrow's Child by Rubem A. Alves. Copyright (c) 1972 by Rubem A. Alves. Used by permission of HarperCollins Publishers.
- "But I don't want to go among mad people" – Lewis Carroll, *Alice in Wonderland*
- "Fighting Absurdity – Albert Camus - The Plague
- John 16:31
- Reflection

Day 28 – New Ways of Seeing
- "The Value of Errors" – William Least Heat Moon, *Blue Highways (A Journey Into America)*, Little, Brown and Company, Boston/Toronto, 1982, pp. 215-216.
- "A Man Becomes His Attentions" – William Least Heat Moon, *Blue Highways (A Journey Into America)*, Little, Brown and Company, Boston/Toronto, 1982., p. 17.
- Matthew 9:14-17, Revelation 21:5-6, II Corinthians 5:16-20
- Reflection

Day 29 – Strangers and Sojourners
- "Finding Meaning In The Journey" – William Least Heat Moon, *Blue Highways (A Journey Into America)*, Little, Brown and Company, Boston/Toronto, 1982, pp. 32, 188.
- "O To Realize Space" – Walt Whitman
- "Plain and Simple" – from Plain and Simple by Sue Bender. Copyright (c) 1989 by Sue Bender. Used by permission of HarperCollins Publishers.
- "I'm Just A Poor, Wayfaring Stranger" – Traditional American Folk Hymn
- Hebrews 11:13-16
- Reflection

index of readings

Day 30 - The Human Being Awaits His Beseiger
- "The Siege of Elly" – from Weapons and Hope by Freeman J. Dyson. Copyright (c) 1984 by Freeman J. Dyson. Used by permission of HarperCollins Publishers.
- "The Hound of Heaven" – Francis Thompson
- Romans 5:6-11
- Reflection

Day 31 - The Great Roles Are Prosaic
- "If He Knows Himself To Be Responsible" – Peter F. Drucker, *Landmarks Of Tomorrow*, Harper and Row, New York, 1957, pp. 269-270. Used by permission of The Peter F. Drucker 1996 Literary Works Trust. All rights reserved.
- Unknown Selection – John Gardiner, *Excellence*, Harper and Row, New York, 1961, p. 154.
- "I Am Only One" – Edward Everett Hale
- Matthew 23:11-12, Matthew 25:31-46, Luke 9:46-48
- Reflection

Day 32 - Unfreakability: The Art of Quieting The Mind
- "Freaking Out" – W. Timothy Gallwey, *The Inner Game of Tennis*, Random House, New York, 1974, p. 131. Used by permission of W. Timothy Gallwey. All rights reserved.
- "If" – Rudyard Kipling
- "A Mighty Fortress Is Our God" – Martin Luther, 1529
- Psalm 46, Isaiah 30:15
- Reflection

Day 33 - Giving And Receiving
- "In Giving Lies A Power" – Samuel Johnson Lindamood
- Deuteronomy 15:7-8, Mark 12:41-44, Luke 12:27-34, James 2:1-6, 14-17, Acts 20:35
- Reflection

Day 34 - Growing Old Gracefully
- "Women See Death Differently" – Charlotte Painter, *Gifts Of Age*, Chronicle Books, San Francisco, p. 1. Used by permission of Charlotte Painter. All rights reserved.
- "Cowards Die Many Times Before Their Deaths" – William Shakespeare
- "Each Man Goes Home Before He Dies" – From ALL THE STRANGE HOURS: THE EXCAVATION OF A LIFE by Loren Eiseley. Copyright © 1975 by Loren Eiseley. Reprinted with the permission of Scribner, a division of Simon & Schuster, Inc. All rights reserved.
- "Age" – Ruth Greig (Age 94)
- Ecclesiates 12:1-8
- Reflection

Day 35 - The Compassionate Beast
- "It Doesn't Behoove Us" – Anonymous
- "The Heresy Of Faith In Human Nature" – from The Parables of Peanuts by Robert L. Short. Text copyright (c) 1968 by Robert L. Short. Cover design and cartoons as arranged in book copyright (c) 1968 by United Feature Syndicate, Inc.. Used by permission of HarperCollins Publishers.
- "All men have a mind which cannot bear to see the sufferings of others" - *Mencius*, trans. James Legge
- Romans 3:10-18
- Jeremiah 13:23
- John 3:3-4
- Reflection

Day 36 - The Will Of God
- "A Different View Of Providence" – Robert A. Raines, *Success Is A Moving Target*, Word Books, Waco, Texas, 1975, pp. 20-21. Used by permission of Robert A. Raines. All rights reserved.
- "The Map Of Life" – From THE ROAD LESS TRAVELED by M. Scott Peck, M.D. Copyright © 1978 M. Scott Peck. Reprinted with the permission of Touchstone, a division of Simon & Schuster, Inc. All rights reserved.
- "To A Waterfowl" – William Cullen Bryant
- Romans 5:1-5, Romans 8:28-31, Romans 12:1-2
- Philippians 2:12-13, James 4:13-15
- Reflection

Day 37 - The Wonder Of Grace
- "Amazing Grace" – John Newton, 1779
- Numbers 6:22-27, John 3:16-18
- Romans 5:6-8, I Corinthians

217

index of readings

15:10, Titus 2:11-14, Ephesians 1:2, Ephesians 2:4-10
- Reflection

Day 38 - The Struggle For Security Knows No Seasons
- Deuteronomy 28:1-6
- Psalm 91, Psalm 127:1-2, Psalm 40:1-3, Psalm 23, Proverbs 10, 9-12, Ephesians 6:11-17
- Reflection

Day 39 - Wrestling Through To God
- "Engagement And Disengagement" – John A. T. Robinson, Honest To God, The Westminster Press, Philadelphia, 1963, pp. 96-98.
- "Practicing The Presence of God" – Brother Lawrence, The Practice Of The Presence Of God, Fleming H. Revell Company, New York, 1895, pp. 16-17.
- Genesis 32:22-32
- Matthew 6:5-13, Matthew 22:39-46, Romans 8:26-27
- Reflection

Day 40 - On Keeping On Keeping On
- Romans 5:1-5; II Corinthians 4:7-12,16-18; Galatians 6:7-9; James 1:2-4, 12; Hebrews 12:1-7
- Reflection

THE SUNDAYS IN LENT

First Sunday In Lent
Day 41 - The Process Of Taming
- "He that is they friend indeed" - Richard Barnfield
- "There Are Men Too Gentle To Live Among Wolves" – James Kavanaugh, There Are Men Too Gentle To Live Among Wolves
- John 1:35-51, John 15:7-17
- Reflection

Second Sunday In Lent
Day 42 - The Salt Of The Earth, Not The Honey Of The Hill
- "Salt Stings" – From THE DIARY OF A COUNTRY PRIEST by Georges Bernanos; translated from the French by Pamela Morris. Copyright © 1937, 1965 by the Macmillan Company. Reprinted with the permission of Scribner, a division of Simon & Schuster, Inc. All rights reserved.
- The Grace Of The Debonaire – Dana Prom Smith, The Debonaire Disciple, © 1973 Dana Prom Smith. Used by permission of Augsburg Fortress Publishers. All rights reserved.
- Matthew 5:13, John 15:18-20
- Reflection

Third Sunday In Lent
Day 43 - There Is No Separation
- "Katherine and Dinah Leave For Boarding School" – from Now and Then by Frederick Buechner. Copyright (c) 1983 by Frederick Buechner. Used by permission of HarperCollins Publishers.
- "We Abhor Separation" – Excerpt(s) from THE HABIT OF LOVING by Barbara Lazear Ascher, copyright © 1986, 1987, 1989 by Barbara Lazear Ascher. Used by permission of Random House, an imprint and division of Penguin Random House LLC. All rights reserved.
- Romans 8:15-18, 31, 35, 37-39
- Romans 6:5-11
- Reflection

Fourth Sunday In Lent
Day 44 - Mysterium Tremendum
- "A Strangely Beautiful Interior" – Excerpt(s) from IN SEARCH OF SCHRODINGER'S CAT: QUANTAM PHYSICS AND REALITY by John Gribbin, copyright © 1984 by John and Mary Gribbin. Used by permission of Bantam Books, an imprint of Random House, a division of Penguin Random House LLC. All rights reserved.
- "Mysterium Tremendum" – Rudolph Otto, The Idea Of The Holy, Oxford University Press, London, 1923, pp. 12-13.
- "God's Grandeur" – Gerald Manley Hopkins
- Isaiah 6:1-8
- Reflection

Passion Sunday
Day 45 - Don't Neglect The Blood
- "Affirming The Love That Suffers" – from Now and Then by Frederick Buechner. Copyright (c) 1983 by Frederick Buechner. Used by permission of HarperCollins Publishers.

index of readings

- "There Is A Fountain Filled With Blood" – William Cowper, 1771, *Hymns For The Living Church* #230, Hope Publishing Company, 1974.
- Matthew 26:26-29, II Samuel 23:13-17, Philippians 2:5-11
- Reflection

Palm Sunday
Day 46 – Choosing Means Renouncing
- "Choosing Means Renouncing" –from The Meaning of Persons by Paul Tournier. Translated by Edwin Hudson. Copyright (c) 1957 by Paul Tournier, renewed (c) 1985 SCM Press Ltd. Used by permission of HarperCollins Publishers.
- "It's Hard To Eliminate Choices" – from Plain and Simple by Sue Bender. Copyright (c) 1989 by Sue Bender. Used by permission of HarperCollins Publishers.
- "The Steep Ascent" – Excerpt from THE STEEP ASCENT by Anne Morrow Lindbergh. Copyright © 1944 and renewed 1971 by Anne Morrow Lindbergh. Reprinted by permission of Houghton Mifflin Harcourt Publishing Company. All rights reserved.
- Deuteronomy 30:15-20, 1 Kings 18:21
- Matthew 6:24; Revelation 3:15-16, 20; Matthew 26:50
- Reflection

Easter Sunday
Day 47 – The Miracle Of Metamorphosis
- "The Monarch Butterfly" – from Infinite in All Directions by Freeman J. Dyson. Copyright (c) 1988, 2004 by Freeman J. Dyson. Used by permission of HarperCollins Publishers.
- "Purgatorio" – Dante, *Purgatorio*, Canto 10
- "The Worms Go In, The Worms Go Out" – Scout Camp Song
- I Corinthians 15:35-44
- Reflection

SUBSTITUTE DAYS

Substitute Day 1
Day 48 – The Denizens Of The Night
- The Theology of Sleep – John Baillie, The Theology Of Sleep (A Sermon), *Christian Devotion*, Charles Scribner's Sons, New York, 1962, p. 102. Used by permission of Oxford University Press. All rights reserved.
- The Denizens of The Night – Samuel Johnson Lindamood
- "Weary with toil, I haste me to bed" Shakespeare, Sonnet 27
- Psalm 4:8 (KJV), Psalm 127:1-2 (KJV)
- Matthew 8:23-27, Luke 23:46
- Reflection

Substitute Day 2
Day 49 – When You Can't Find The Tiger
- In Search Of My Foundations – Excerpt(s) from THE HABIT OF LOVING by Barbara Lazear Ascher. copyright © 1986, 1987, 1989 by Barbara Lazear Ascher. Used by permission of Random House, an imprint and division of Penguin Random House LLC. All rights reserved.
- When You Can't Find The Tiger – Robert A Raines, *Success Is A Moving Target*, Word Books, Waco, Texas, 1975, pp. 17, 23.
- Matthew 6:25-34
- Reflection

Substitute Day 3
Day 50 – Beyond Astonishment
- Luke 1:26-38, Matthew 1:18-25
- Hebrews 11:32-40
- Reflection

photography credits

Beauty in the Ordinary features the creative work of numerous talented photographers. All photographs are in the public domain or governed by creative commons or royalty free licenses.

Opening prayer: Candle hands - Myriams-Fotos

Day 1: Cigarette package - Ben Wildman; Train tracks and regret - sreza24595

Day 2: Purple water - Susan-lu4esm; Sunglasses with tangled hair - veeterzy

Day 3: Running away - Mr. Music; Busy subway - Karen Lau

Day 4: Colorful Child - Senjuti Kundu

Day 5: Lonely water - Free-Photos; River and man - Free-Photos

Day 6: Escalator out of service - Ben Wildman; Escalator and Light - Free-Photos

Day 7: Helicopter and blue sky - Ben Wildman; Motorcycle and rider - SplitShire

Day 8: Sunset levitation - Steve Halama; Spiritual illumination - Stefan Keller

Day 9: Homeless man on sidewalk - Ben Wildman; Jim Crow water fountain - WikiImages

Day 10: Woman eating ice cream - Josh Pereira; Gold coins - image4you

Day 11: Funky winking child - Tong Nguyen

Day 12: Fake shark - Wachiraphorn Thongya; Fake ostrich - analogicus

Day 13: Girlfriends in blue - jacejojo; Slum children - billycm

Day 14: Island aerial view - Oliver Sjostro

Day 15: Homeless man, head in hand - Leroy_Skalstad; Wall of luggage - Caroline Selfors

Day 16: Children with flower - Bessi; Elderly couple arm in arm - Mabel Amber

Day 17: Headlamps below the Milky Way - Noel Bauza; Dreamer - Leandro DeCarvalho

Day 18: Comforting hug - Prostock-Studio; Firefighters with smoke - skeeze

Day 19: Cancer couple - Photographee.eu; Lighting candles - pixel2013

Day 20: Kneading dough - AdinaVoicu; Steaming apple pie - Finn-b

Day 21: Lost in mist - Free-Photos; House in ruin - Herbert2512

Day 22: Carmel sundae - Kobby Mendez; Woman with 3D glasses - Sarah Wolfe

Day 23: Gravestone - Ben Wildman; Skull - ApeWithCamera

Day 24: Stained glass - Magda Ehlers

Day 25: Suicide pills - Sharon McCutcheon; Sailboat sky - jplenio

Day 26: Skyscraper clouds - Free-Photos; Turtle - Free-Photos

Day 27: Absurd banana - RyanMcGuire

Day 28: Crab Nebula - WikiImages; Hubble telescope - Andrew-Art

Day 29: Homeless man feeding dog - Leroy_Skalstad; Cabin in woods - 12019

Day 30: Fortress from below - christels

Day 31: Mom kissing little girl - 5540867; Tree planting - annaelizaearl

Day 32: Stacked rocks - Bekir Donmez

Day 33: Wrapped gift - HakinMhan; Flowers through fence - Klimkin

Day 34: Smiling old lady - Free-Photos; Dignified old man - Pexels

Day 35: Man with flower hat - Daria Rem; Angel and demon - gunthersimmermacher

Day 36: Sanctuary - Ben Wildman

Day 37: Lotus flower - pieonane; Light rays in chapel - Skitterphpto

Day 38: Suit of armor - Pexels; Boy sitting with teddy bear - Pixabay

Day 39: Church with ivy - Ben Wildman;

Day 40: Running steps - Clique Images; Exasperated girl - Henrikke Due

Day 41: Cat with bandana - Jae Park; Pug in blanket - Free-Photos

Day 42: Spices on spoons - Calum Lewis; Honey dripping - Mae Mu

Day 43: Crying girl - Arwan Sutanto; Grave with cross - Kenny Orr

Day 44: Tree with roots and light - Jeremy Bishop; Tree in bloom - Meric Dagli

Day 45: Crucifixion - solarilucho; Eucharist and tablecloth - hudsoncrafted

Day 46: Two paths in the woods - Vladislav Babienko; Two paths gravel - Jon Tyson

Day 47: Chrysalis butterfly emerging - GLady; Monarch butterfly - Kathy Servian

Day 48: Milky Way at night - Gabriele Motter; Sleepy koala - Pexels

Day 49: Overwhelmed by sticky notes - Luis Villasmil ; Lost among sand dunes - Dan Grinwis

Day 50: Galaxy and water - Pexels; Nativity scene - Walter Chavez

www.ingramcontent.com/pod-product-compliance
Lightning Source LLC
Chambersburg PA
CBHW040611120526
44589CB00043B/51